Ethnics and Enclaves
Boston's Italian North End

Studies in
American History and Culture, No. 31

Robert Berkhofer, Series Editor

Director of American Culture Programs
and Richard Hudson Research Professor of History
The University of Michigan

Other Titles in This Series

Ethnics and Enclaves
Boston's Italian North End

WITHDRAWN

by
William M. De Marco

UMI RESEARCH PRESS
Ann Arbor, Michigan

Produced and distributed by
UMI Research Press
an imprint of
University Microfilms International
Ann Arbor, Michigan 48106

Library of Congress Cataloging in Publication Data

DeMarco, William M.
Ethnics and enclaves.

(Studies in American history and culture ; no. 31)
Revision of thesis (Ph.D.)–Boston College, 1980.
Bibliography: p.
Includes index.
1. Italian Americans–Massachusetts–Boston. 2. Boston
(Mass.)–Social life and customs. 3. North End (Boston,
Mass.)–Social life and customs. I. Title. II. Series.

| F73.9.I8D45 1980 | 974.4'6100451 | 81-16508 |
| ISBN 0-8357-1251-6 | | AACR2 |

This work is dedicated to the memory of my father, who died just three months prior to its completion. His life was a living example of the meaning of the Italian Family, and, for this, I am eternally grateful.

Contents

List of Illustrations

Figures

Maps

Plates

List of Tables

Preface

A tourist passing through the North End of Boston in 1981 is confronted with a pleasant melange of the ancient and the agreeable. Historic structures, lit by centuries-old lanterns, preside over cobbled passageways, welcoming tens of thousands of Americans in search of their past. Enroute to some of America's most hallowed shrines, these tourists enter a living ethnic neighborhood which testifies as fully to America's past as do the sacred structures they came to see. The fine restaurants, pastry shops, and cafes, as well as the outwardly affectionate camaraderie of the residents, the oft-heard Italian dialects, and captivating aromas of homemade Italian regional delicacies give the visitor a feeling of pleasure and a desire to return time and again.

The quality of life of the area's residents generally seems quite pleasant. Early nineteenth-century warehouses have become luxury ocean-front condominiums. Low-cost tenements have been made into modern apartments. A dilapidated 150-year-old marketplace has been transformed wondrously into a unique shopping arcade, complete with a revitalized open market and new sidewalk cafes. Existing parks have been refurbished, and a new waterfront park, complete with trellised arcade, has been built.

This contemporary image of the North End portrays two fallacies, however, of which I became all too aware in 1958. First, the North End of today does not accurately reflect that same community of nearly a century ago, and, second, these individuals did not and do not today perceive themselves as Italians, but rather as Italian members of distinct subcultures.

Recent urban renewal has restored the facade of many of the buildings of a former era, but has not recaptured the very poor quality of life which characterized this immigrant neighborhood a century ago.[1] During the mid and late nineteenth century, the North End was known as a tenement community, where the destitute lived in squalid overcrowded conditions—the most crowded one hundred acres of land on earth in 1900. A lack of adequate sanitation contributed to a high rate of disease. The moral ills of alcoholism and lasciviousness were greatly aided by the presence of one tavern for every two acres of habitable space, and more resident whores than resident physicians. The neighborhood became the home of the poorest of immigrants to our shores. Notably an Irish and Jewish neighborhood by 1880, the North End had long been identified as an undesirable residence by middle and upper-class Americans by the time the Italians settled there in any great numbers.

This was the neighborhood which Professor James Serpe, a Loyola University (Chicago) historian described more than twenty years ago. That lecture began with the following statement: "Today, we will discuss a classic American slum: the Italian neighborhood in the North End of Boston."[2] That statement quickened the adrenalin, and elicited an indignant protest within me. Everything he was about to say reflected a perception which was contrary to the experience of my North End Italian youth. True, the main thorough-fares of the community had been crowded, but not to the degree he described, I reasoned. I remembered that the neighborhood had been dirty, but nowhere nearly as dirty as the picture he painted. Nor did I agree with his description of violence in the North End. Upon reflection, I asked, had I just been fooling myself, out of a false sense of loyalty? I soon began to think that perhaps I had been too close a part of the community to realize just what sort of place it really was. However, this moment of objectivity quickly dissipated when not once did he mention the "Sicilian section" or "Avellinese section," nor the fierce and exclusive loyalty members of each Catholic Church had to their local parish. He always talked of "the Italians," but never once mentioned that Italian provincial loyalties in the North End were exclusionary. Friction between Italians and the residual Irish population remaining in the community was stressed, but where was the description of the violence which often erupted between individuals of different Italian regions? He described Italians who spoke "a" foreign language, but failed to mention that all Italians spoke their regional dialects.

Like the contemporary visitor to the North End, Professor Serpe perceived what was most apparent, but was incapable of understanding what he saw. The North End was not the home of "Italians," for the local residents did not perceive themselves as such. It was the location of individuals from the Italian peninsula, who identified themselves as belonging to a particular province or village in Italy. They turned to their individual provincial customs and dialects with fierce pride and loyalty, often even into the third generation, living in subcultural enclaves to the present day.

The retention of old-world customs and creation of enclaves are not unique to the North End of Boston, but are widespread practices throughout the many "Little Italys" of America. As early as 1921, Robert Park and Herbert Miller noted, in their classic study *Old World Traits Transplanted,* the existence of geographically-based enclaves in the "Little Italy" near New York's Bowery. They further observed that Sicilians from the town of Cinisi were concentrated in midtown Manhattan, and that those from Avigliano

(Basilicata) clustered in East Harlem.[3] Their study was partly inspired by Jacob Riis's 1898 article "Out of Mulberry Street: Stories of Tenement Life in New York City,"[4] in which a similar enclave pattern had been observed among Calabrians. In this case, Riis observed that Calabrians on Mulberry Street grouped according to their town of origin. Twenty years later, another scholar revealed that a similar pattern existed in the smaller New York city of Utica. There, the great majority of Italians came from Laurenzana and adjacent towns in Basilicata.[5] In Norristown, Pennsylvania, Ianni and Huganir identified a significant enclave of individuals from Sciacca, a town in Girgenti, Sicily. This was the most prominent enclave in an Italian district dominated by subcultures.[6] In 1942, Charles Churchill wrote that Southern Italians from different villages had settled in different parts of New Jersey, creating transplanted communities.[7] New Haven, Connecticut had two distinct Italian neighborhoods: one made up of immigrants from the mountain provinces, and the other occupied by individuals from the Salerno area, mostly the towns of Amalfi and Scafati Atani.[8] In neighboring Middletown, Connecticut, most of the Italians came from the Sicilian town of Melilli, in the province of Siracusa.[9] A Connecticut study [10] shows that most Stamford Italians came from two Italian towns, and lived in clearly delineated enclaves. The towns in question were Santo Mango sul Calore in Campania and Avigliano in Potenza. Even the large midwestern cities of Cleveland, Milwaukee, and Chicago witnessed the creation of Italian subcultural enclaves. Termini Imerense in Palermo, Sicily, was responsible for Cleveland's largest concentration of Italians.[11] Sicily's northern coastal towns between Palermo and Milazzo sent their sons and daughters to Milwaukee's "Little Italy."[12] In Chicago, the largest Italian neighborhoods were created by enclaves of Sicilians from Altavilla Milicia, Bagheria Vicari, Monreale, and Termini Imerense in Palermo.[13]

In spite of these numerous citations only recently has the phenomenon of what Amos Hawley called "cultural enclaves"[14] been widely analyzed. Oscar Handlin, in *Immigration in American Life: A Reappraisal,* called these cultural enclaves "functional equivalents" of the village and family network.[15] John and Leatrice MacDonald brought Handlin's evaluation one step further, when they found that these cultural enclaves, created as functional equivalents for the villages and family network, were sustained by "chain migration" and "chain occupation processes"[16] (earlier immigrants encouraged other family members to migrate and helped locate employment for them). In 1962, Herbert J. Gans, while writing about Boston's West End Italians, observed that "a review of three generations *may* (italics mine) suggest that . . . their environment has not really changed as drastically as it appears."[17] Because his study was more concerned with urban renewal of the West End rather than its ethnic groups (devoting only three pages in his entire study to the latter), Gans failed adequately to develop what my research shows was a correct observation.

The identification of Italian ethnic enclaves has not yet been undertaken for Boston's North End, which truly has one of the most closely knit and unadulterated "Italian" ethnic communities in America. The objective of this work is to examine these North End "enclaves;" the extent to which they were caused by a search for "functional equivalents" and fed by "chain migration" and "chain occupation processes." I accomplished this by examining the *housing, marriage, religious,* and *employment* patterns within the North End Italian community during the years of its greatest Italian occupancy. Besides offering a new working of existing data, this study provides the reader with an interpretation which reflects closely the values of the members of the North End Italian community. This is reinforced by an extensive use of oral history and is supported by new collections of marriage and employment data. Unlike Robert Wood's *Americans in Process,* an outsider's view of Boston's ethnic neighborhoods, this is a study written from within the community. The four areas of housing, marriage, religion, and employment have been chosen because they represent the most important elements of Italian-American existence: the preeminence of the family and a respect for old-world values. They have also been chosen because supporting data, though hitherto undeveloped, were available for analysis.

Mine is not a chronological study of the North End,[18] nor is it an in-depth study of the North End Italian community. Instead, it is a case study in which old-world values are identified, and their retention is analyzed. The North End Italian community is the social laboratory in which this study takes place.

Acknowledgments

I would like to express my sincerest appreciation to both the administration and faculty of Boston College, without whose generosity and support this work would never have become a reality. Professor Thomas O'Connor of the History Department was of immeasurable assistance in all phases of this work, offering particularly valuable assistance with the maps presented here. Professor Alan Reinerman oversaw the development of material related to modern Italian history, and Professor Seymour Leventman offered direction in the field of ethnicity. Professor Paul Spagnoli's assistance with the statistical data presented here greatly aided in defining the limits of the present study, and gave direction to my future research. A special debt of gratitude is reserved for Professor Andrew Buni, whose encouragement and dedication are responsible for whatever is of merit in these pages.

Many scholars from the American Italian Historical Association (AIHA) were kind enough to offer advice at all phases of research. Professor Frank Femminella, State University of New York (Albany) spent long hours reviewing the early stages of research, and made many valuable suggestions concerning the role of the family in Italian life. Professor Betty Boyd Caroli, City University of New York (Queens College) offered suggestions concerning Italian repatriation, and further bibliographic development. Professor Robert Harney, Multicultural History Society of Ontario, University of Toronto, shared some of his most recent research findings concerning labor agents. Professor Luciano Iorizzo, State University of New York (Oswego) made appropriate suggestions concerning the role of *padroni* among Italian-Americans. Professor George Pozzetta, University of Florida, greatly aided in the refinement of the present study by his encouragement that I participate in the 1978 AIHA conference in Toronto, Canada.

This work would never have been completed without the generosity of the Immigration History Research Center, University of Minnesota. As a 1977 IHRC Grant Recipient, I was permitted to study their extensive collection. This greatly aided in the identification of primary source material. Their collection of Italian newspapers was particularly valuable. Special mention must be made of the scholarly advice and assistance offered by Professor Rudolph Vecoli, the Center's Director. His scholarship and support have made a profound impact on the quality of my research.

The Center for Migration Studies, Staten Island, New York, has been very generous in its support of my research, permitting me to be a Scholar in Residence on three separate occasions since 1976. Their collections concerning Italian National Churches was of particular assistance. The Center's Archivist, Dr. Ola della Cava, offered advice concerning North End Italian religious life. Dr. Lydio Tomasi, the Center's Director, made appropriate suggestions concerning my research at all phases of development.

Dr. Silvano Tomasi, the Editor of *International Migration Review,* read my manuscript in both its early and final forms. His recommendations have greatly aided in the development of the present research, and the identification of future areas of study. Dr. Gianfausto Rosoli, Director of *Centro Studi Emigrazione,* Rome, Italy, kindly read my manuscript and made suggestions concerning the analysis of the marriage data presented here.

A debt of gratitude must be expressed to Rev. Bede Ferrara, O.F.M., pastor of Saint Leonard's Church, and Rev. Hillary Zanon, C.M., pastor of Sacred Heart Church, for permitting me to study their respective Sacramental Files. Mrs. Mary Brady of the Chancery Office of the Catholic Archdiocese of Boston was very helpful in locating church records which were of particular value to my study of the Società San Marco. I would also like to thank Rev. William Wolkovich, a scholar and friend, for his advice and assistance with the preparation of this manuscript.

I am very grateful to the many North End residents (see Appendix) who generously participated in this research. I would like to specifically thank Miss Pietrina Maravigna for years of encouragement and support. In addition, I would particularly like to thank those people who allowed me to reproduce irreplaceable family snapshots in this book. Although the quality of reproduction is the best available to us there are, of course, imperfections. The editors and I have elected to include them nonetheless, in the belief that they are of sufficient interest to offset their physical drawbacks.

A very special debt of gratitude is owed to my wife and children, whose love and encouragement made this work possible.

1

A Nation for Convenience Sake

In order better to understand the Italian need for "enclaves" in the North End of Boston, it is first necessary to look at the root causes of Italian emigration. Individuals who migrated from the Italian peninsula and Sicily at the turn of the century were conveniently referred to as "Italians" by host societies. This perception erroneously implied that these immigrants shared more than a common political national identity. In point of fact, these "Italians" shared neither a common language nor culture, and did not perceive of themselves as "Italians."[1] The relatively recent unification of Italy in 1861 failed to mollify centuries of mistrust and hostility between northern and southern Italians. Northern Italians disparaged their southern counterparts for centuries, often viewing their customs as primitive.[2] These prejudices were deeply rooted and most often bore racial overtones.[3] The fact that northern Italians were of Germanic and French stock, and that southern Italians were descendants of Greeks, Turks, and Africans, entered into the equation. While northern Italians were generally considered cosmopolitan, educated, and financially more secure, southern Italians were usually characterized as parochial, illiterate, and bound to the soil.

Most of the Italians who migrated to Boston's North End since 1870 were from the southern Italian regions of Campania, and Sicily (see map 1). Both regions, the largest in southern Italy, continually suffered from the natural disasters of cholera, drought, earthquake, and volcanic eruption for centuries. During that same period, man-made disasters which accompany warfare also took their toll. Campania knew almost unabated foreign conquest since pre-Roman times, being successively occupied by Hirpini, Roman, Goth, Byzantine, Lombard, Norman, Hohenstaufen, Aragonese, Hapsburg and Bourbon forces. Sicily suffered a similar fate with Phoenician, Cartaginian, Greek, Roman, Byzantine, Arab, Norman, Hohenstaufen, Aragonese, Hapsburg, and Bourbon forces occupying her borders for nearly 2,500 years.

This combination of centuries of natural and man-made disasters caused southern Italians to learn to rely solely on their "family unit" for survival. The Italian *contadino* (peasant) developed an intricate network of relationships within *la famiglia* (the family). This network is described as a hierarchy by Famminella and Quadagno:

> The first category was *la famiglia* and consisted of blood relationships, family members to whom one owed all his loyalty. *La famiglia* was supplemented by *comparagio,* or godparents, who comprised the second category in the hierarchy. Casual acquaintances and those whose family status demanded respect made up the third category in the hierarchy. Finally, there were *stranieri,* which included all other people such as shopkeepers and fellow workers who were objects of suspicion and, as such, kept at a distance.[4]

La famiglia was nominally a patriarchal system.[5] The father, as the head of the family, was responsible for arbitrating all family disputes, and making all decisions which had a bearing on *la famiglia's* relationship with the outside world. He supported the family by the sweat of his brow, thus keeping the family out of poverty. The amount of food he was able to provide was a yardstick of his worth. Provider or not, the father was always to be respected because of his preeminent position in the family structure.

The mother managed all the internal affairs of the family. As the keeper of the hearth, which was the source of all that gave meaning to life, she "managed all financial affairs, and arranged marriages of her children, which were critical for survival of *la via vecchia* (the old way). In a world in which the family status was judged not by the occupation of the father but by the signs of well-being that emanated from the household, the mother played an important role in securing that status."[6]

La via vecchia, or the old way, became the value system which protected the members of *la famiglia* from all misfortune. The perpetuation of these customs was all-important. To the southern Italian, a well-educated person was one who was properly schooled in what the family considered to be proper conduct. Thus, to be *ben educato* (well educated) often implied an ignorance of formal education because teachers were *stranieri* and, as such, ignorant of the family ways.[7] Hard physical work was viewed as a positive good because it prepared a son for the familiar responsibilities of manhood, and a daughter for her role as a woman within the family unit. The greatest of all offences was disrespect for one's family. A Sicilian proverb says: "He who is obedient to father and mother will live happily and prosper." A person who violated *la via vecchia* was an outcast of both family and community.

Because of the all-embracing importance of *la famiglia,*[8] the village which housed that family had a very special significance to the southern Italian. The village *campanile* (church bell) became a symbol of that relationship of village to family. The unique sound of the village bell not only announced all the important family events but, as time went by, defined the boundaries of the village. Those beyond the sound of the bell were *stranieri* (foreigners to the family unit), to be trusted even less than the nonfamily members from within the village community. The term *campanilismo* (that which is within the sound of the village churchbell) describes this complex relationship.

These village communities, or "rural cities"[9] as Vecoli calls them, because of their geographic isolation, history of subservience, and familial old ways, developed distinct manners, traditions, values, and dress. Geographical proximity failed to act as a catalyst for neighboring communities. This may have been so because villages often developed distinct dialects, which perpetuated local customs, and further alienated the already unwanted *stranieri*. Though these dialects generally shared much in common within the same province, in some cases intercommunication even in neighboring villages became very difficult. For example, in Italian the word for "celery" is *sedono*, in Neapolitan, *alaccia;* "witch" is *maga* in Italian, *iannara* in Neapolitan, *donna di fuora* in Sicilian. In some cases, words are similar. For example, "more" in Italian is *piu', chiu'* in Neapolitan. "Beautiful" is *bello* in Italian and *beddu* in Sicilian. The word for "onion" in Italian is *cipolla,* while in the neighboring towns of Randazzo and Girgenti in Sicily it is *cipulli* and *cipudda* respectively. Ignazio Silone of Fontamara in Abruzzi seemed to be speaking for all southern Italians when he wrote as late as 1924:

> Let no one get into his head that Fontamarens speak Italian. The Italian language is for us a foreign language, a dead language, a language whose vocabulary and grammar have grown complex without remaining in touch with us, our way of living, our way of acting, our way of thinking, or our way of expressing ourselves. . . . If it is true that to express oneself well in any language one must learn to think in it, then the trouble we have in speaking this Italian clearly must mean that we do not know how to think in it, and that this Italian culture is a foreign one to us.[10]

For centuries, Italians have not identified themselves as such. Margaret Carlyle, describing this very issue, explained: "They belonged not to Italy but first to their families and then to their villages."[11] Boston's Italian immigrants were no different than those other millions who settled in the United States from 1870 to 1930. Boston became the new home of predominantly Campanians, Sicilians and Abruzzesi who retained all of the parochial values which characterized their life in the old world. From their perspective, they were different peoples, just as Americans are different from Australians or Rhodesians.

Since the family unit was so tightly woven in southern Italy, the push factors which caused significant Italian migration at the turn of the century must have been very strong. Each emigrant experienced a personal crisis which allowed but one solution. The solution was so radical that it not only caused an abandonment of the sacred village, but also brought about at least a temporary separation from the family. In an attempt to build a bridge between the old world and the new, Italians eagerly sought out *paesani* (fellow villagers) from their old village or province upon arrival in America. In the North End of Boston, individuals lived in "enclaves,"[12] in an attempt to help lessen the pain of loss. In time, more family members would join the earlier emigrants, and the sacred *la via vecchia* would be restored in a new but more desirable environment.

When Italians settled in Boston's North End at the turn of the century, old-world values, particularly among southerners, may have been felt more strongly than at any time in recent generations. Centuries of reliance on *la famiglia* and *la via vecchia,* as well as identification with *campanilismo,* were made more significant by the failures of the nineteenth-century movement to restructure Italian political and social life, popularly known as the *Risorgimento.* This nineteenth-century movement for the unification of Italy was the first major attempt to restructure Italian society in centuries. As such, it built up hopes of reform throughout the Italian peninsula. A continuation of North-South hostilities, the remoteness of the government, and a continually deteriorating landlord-tenant farmer relationship, frustrated dreams of reform among the *contadini* (southern peasant class), and brought about a further retrenchment of the old ways (*la via vecchia*). The factors which "pushed" Italian migrants to the North End enclaves at the turn of the century, and the values they brought with them, can only be understood in light of the frustrations experienced by these *contadini* at the hands of nineteenth and early twentieth-century Italian lawmakers. Virtually every aspect of their lives was shaped by them. For this reason a brief description of nineteenth and early twentieth-century Italian political and social history is essential here.

Through the centuries, Italian history has been influenced inexorably by the Catholic Church. The nineteenth-century was no exception. The Roman Pontiff and the Papal States were viewed by most contemporaries[13] as the major obstacle to reforms brought about by a secular unified Italy. The *Risorgimento* was viewed as a crusade which the Catholic Church seemed determined to prevent if it meant the dissolution of the Papal States. Colorful figures, such as Giuseppe Mazzini, Camillo Benso di Cavour, Guiseppe Garibaldi, and even King Victor Emmanuel of Piedmont, became folk heroes in various European cities, while Pius IX increasingly emerged as the obstacle to secular unification. In the post-Rousseau world of Marx and Darwin, the Catholic Church was already viewed by many as an obsolete institution which might at best be tolerated, but certainly not catered to. Cynicism had become agnosticism for many intellectuals of the period, who were already predisposed to condemn any attempt at Italian self-determination and reform. The ascendency of Giovanni Cardinal Mastai-Ferretti to the papacy as Pius IX[14] in 1846 did as much to dampen their spirits as it did to convince the pro-papal faction, known as "neo-Geulfs," that an Italy unified under the papacy would soon be a reality.

The liberal reforms which the new pope introduced into the Papal States from 1846 to 1848 reverberated throughout Italy. Messina, Sicily, which would send significant numbers of its population to the North End later in the century, suffered a major bombardment in 1848 at the hands of its own ruler, King Ferdinand II of the Two Sicilies, who was subsequently named *Bomba* (The Bomber) by his Sicilian subjects. Over 15,000 were arrested and tortured in the Messina and Palermo areas.[15] The revolution came anyway.

With both France and Austria manipulating for advantage,[16] Mazzini agitating for a new Roman republic, and Cavour scheming in behalf of the King of Piedmont as the ruler of a unified Italy,[17] the next decade and a half was marked by both social and political turmoil. To most of the southern peasants who cared, only Giuseppe Garibaldi[18] was viewed as an individual capable of improving their lot. The *contadini* of southern Italy accepted Garibaldi's promise of self-rule and redistribution of land more than the word of most foreigners. His widely recognized charismatic personality was in part the basis for this faith. Many *contadini* joined his march northward in hopes of a new life of less poverty, but those peasants of Campania and Sicily would once again have their dreams shattered. Cavour, intent on installing the King of Piedmont as king of a unified Italy, led Garibaldi to believe that a plebiscite in southern Italy supported King Victor Emmanuel as ruler. Garibaldi, bowing to the apparent will of the people, relinquished control of his army to the King of Piedmont, and paid him his allegiance in October, 1860. For the *contadini,* this most recent of invasions of their homeland reaffirmed their long-held conviction that *stranieri,* even when they preached a gospel of equitable land distribution and less poverty, were, after all, foreigners who failed to value and understand *la via vecchia.* Most peasants returned to the security of a *laissez faire* attitude toward government. Some, however, particularly in Sicily and Campania, continued to resist this most recent of invaders. Observing the unnecessary oppression of absentee landlords, ever-increasing taxes, continued military occupancy, and widespread conscription, guerrilla bands continued to resist unification. Had Garibaldi not accepted Cavour's plan, the South may have united into one or more independent nations. Italy's subsequent political history could not possibly have been any less concerned for the welfare of the southern peasant classes.

The southern *contadini* were not the only group which experienced frustration with the structure of the new nation. The Mazzini republicans, the Garibaldi idealists, and the neo-Geulf conservatives had all been thwarted in their attempts to create an Italy molded by the struggles and dreams of many generations. The Cavourian policy of a free Italy, governed by the House of Savoy, won out. Many individuals, Garibaldi among them, took a cautious wait-and-see attitude.[19]

The sudden death of Cavour in 1861 left Italy without a policymaker of stature. Though King Victor Emmanuel II was the head of state, the royal powers were exercised by a ministry responsible to a two-chamber parliament. The House of Savoy, [20] with the possible exception of Eugene of Savoy, was never known for its charismatic offspring. The centuries-old regional differences, the individualism of the Italian personality, the alienation of support by the tradition-laden Catholic Church, and the failure of the new government to provide inspiring leadership moved the war of Italian unification from the battlefield to the Chamber of Deputies.

There were two major political factions in Italy during the period between Italian unification and World War I. The factions known as the *Destra Storica* (Historic Right) and *Sinistra Storica* (Historic Left), controlled Italian political life, and, as a result, Italian emigration during the entire period.

The *Destra Storica,*[21] the party of Cavour, stood for a strong central administration, continuation of ecclesiastical authority within the framework of separation of church and state, considerable power for the head of state, limited suffrage, and sound financial management. To this end, the party attempted to remain somewhat isolated from costly involvement in the most recent military events in central Europe. During its fifteen years in power (1861-1876), the *Destra Storica* achieved many of its goals. It created a national military force, with universal conscription governed by the crown. It must be stressed, however, that this conscription's heaviest burdens were placed on the *contadini* of the South who could not afford to pay the fee which would buy their sons and spouses out of military service. In 1870, it annexed the Papal States to the kingdom. By 1876, four thousand additional miles of rail were added to the mere one thousand which existed in 1861. The *Destra* created a public school system, though universal education was not one of its goals. In Sicily and Campania, where the highest illiteracy rates existed, mutual aid societies run by local citizens inaugurated weekend schools for the laboring class. These *Societa' di Mutuo Soccorso,*[22] which also provided health and welfare services, began as early as 1863 in Sicily.

It must be pointed out that the government, though tolerant of mutual aid societies, viewed them with great suspicion. By 1894, there were 850 such organizations in Campania and Sicily. The pockets of military resistance which still existed in the South after unification were generally placed in the same category as the mutual aid societies—both were "radical" activities which had to be closely watched, and eradicated wherever possible. To this end, the neutralization of the South became one of the major goals of the *Destra*. In 1863, General Govone of Piedmont, a northern aristocrat who had little patience with southern resistance, attempted to put down a rebellion in Sicily by torturing, decimating, and burning out entire villages. Most of this

Map 1. Italy

Map 2. Regions of Italy—Popular Designation of North/South Italy

Map 3. Twenty-six Provinces of Southern Italy, as Identified in
Sacramental Files of North End Italian Churches

activity took place near Messina and Palermo. No doubt Govone recalled similar uprisings in 1848 in Messina, and even as far back as the 1820 revolt in the Province of Avellino in Campania which led to revolts throughout all of southern Italy. The children of these Avellinese and Sicilian residents would constitute the largest group in the North End of Boston by 1900. By 1865, the *Destra* achieved its goal of neutralizing the South. The government permanently stationed more than 120,000 soldiers in the *Mezzogiorno* to guarantee continued loyalty to the crown. While this occupation was classified a military and political success, it only served to create an even greater alienation among the southern peasant class.

The successes of the *Destra* alienated the masses of poor not only because of the military presence but also because of a regressive tax structure which expected southern *contadini* to pay a larger percentage of taxes than their northern counterparts. The centuries-old class system, which placed northern Italians at the top of the hierarchy and Sicilians at the very bottom, was perpetuated beyond the *Risorgimento*. As we shall see, this class system would find its way to the North End of Boston at a later date. Italy's greatest social problem of the late nineteenth and early twentieth centuries was what to do with the *Mezzogiorno*. Emigration proved to be one solution.

On March 18, 1876, the *Destra Storica* was unable to survive a parliamentary crisis. The *Sinistra Storica* came to power. The *Sinistra* was made up of Mazzini republicans and Garibaldians, as well as nonaligned members of Italian society. Some of the more extreme Mazzini republicans formed a coalition with the *Sinistra* upon Mazzini's death in 1872. They were appropriately known as the *Estrema* (extreme). The most prominent leaders of the *Sinistra Storica* were Francesco Crispi, Giuseppe Zanardelli, and Agostino Depretis.

The goals of the *Sinistra* differed greatly from those of its opposition. The *Sinistra* advocated greater suffrage, decentralization of power, the subordination of the executive to the legislative branch, strict anticlerical policies, universal elementary education, a more equitable tax structure, and a foreign policy which would make Italy a world power.[23]

The *Sinistra* soon found it necessary to form a coalition with the *Destra*. The wide divergence of policies was bridged to the point that both parties developed similar programs based on political expediency. Under the *Sinistra's* leadership, the *Mezzogiorno* was still exploited by the North. Church property was confiscated, becoming the property of northern aristocrats. Mortgages were taken on southern land by members of the government, who in turn raised land taxes and passed the burden on to the southern *contadini*. A mule tax was continued. These financial burdens often forced the *contadini* to pay upward of 90 percent of their crops for rent. Taxes were levied on vineyards which were devastated by disease in the 1870s.

Wheat, which had already fallen to a record low of 22 lire per 220 pounds, was taxed, as was salt, which was used as a preservative.

Avellino, in the Region of Campania, about 30 miles east of Naples, known for its vineyards, grains, and sulfur, was particularly affected. Virtually all of its agricultural crops suffered from disease, and its peasant population was expected to absorb the loss by absentee landlords who usually lived in the North. Bread riots broke out throughout Italy in 1880. The Region of Campania again suffered the greatest disaster with over 65 percent of the Naples-Avellino population without work and food by 1881. A cholera epidemic in Naples the following year aggravated an already insufferable situation. Even the prized citrus crop, the pride of parts of Campania and Sicily, suffered from a poor harvest and lowered prices due to foreign competition.[24] The disparity between the standard of living of the North versus the South became an unbridgeable chasm by the mid 1880s. It is little wonder that Boston's Italian immigration, mostly from Campania and Sicily, began in earnest in this decade.

The government's response to the human and financial disaster was to create a commission to study the agricultural conditions of the South.[25] As a result of this investigation, some of the regressive taxes were lessened, but the economy of the region had already suffered a mortal blow.

Francesco Crispi,[26] who was born in Sicily, served as premier from 1887 to 1891, and 1893 to 1896. In spite of his origins, even the Crispi regime was characterized by a lack of empathy for the *Mezzogiorno*. The military, which relied heavily on conscription of southern peasants, was used by Crispi to secure Italy's recognition as a world power. In Ethiopia, he attempted to enforce the terms of the "Treaty of Uccialli" (1889). The Ethiopians humiliated the Italian forces at Adowa in March, 1896, an embarassment which caused a crisis from which the *Sinistra* never recovered. It is ironic that the *Sinistra*, which attempted to provide greater concern for the needs of the lower classes of Italian society initially,[27] is most remembered for bringing the repressive policies of the previous government to new depths of disaster for the South.

The fall of the *Sinistra* as the dominant political force in Italy brought with it eight years of political and social turmoil. In 1904, as a result of these events, George Scigliano,[28] the leading North End Italian politician of the period, writing in the *Boston Traveler,* reflected back on those years and graphically told "Why Italians Emigrate" to the North End Italian community in particular. He wrote in part:

> People who leave their own for another country do so usually because they are dissatisfied with their lot in their native land, and hope to secure a greater measure of happiness under the flag of some other nation.

Italy has been for some years morally as well as temporally one of the most volcanic countries in Europe, and at times conditions there become grave enough to warrant the gloomiest prognostications. The Italian people have suffered untold evils as a result of the tax on food and the failure of the grain supply in the last harvest. There is no prospect of immediately replenishing the food supply, and bread riots become ugly probabilities.

The causes of the chronic trouble in Italy are—ceaseless ambition and obligations, impelling or compelling them to maintain an army proportionate to her allied agreement with the Triple Alliance.

This ambition cost the country dear in two ways—actual taxation for the maintenance of an expensive army, and, even more heavily, in the unforeseen idleness of hundreds of thousands of conscripts undergoing compulsory military service. To collect the taxes, such as those on food and salt, which are extremely unfair and oppressive, it becomes necessary to resort to the sale of farms and fields, thus driving the peasants into starvation, while their sons, dragged away to serve in the army, are unable to earn anything, or to help in tilling the farms or lighten the burden of poverty for their families in any way. Add to this a very costly administration for the luxurious aristocracy to be maintained in splendor and opulence, and the immense drain on the country by the presence of religious orders, and it is not hard to see why Italy is in such a chronic situation.

About a year ago when the formal announcement was made that the Triple Alliance would be renewed, immigration from Italy increased at such an extent, and has continued to increase since then, that in point of immigration, today it is the first country in the world in this category. The steamship service between Boston and Italy was commenced about January, 1900. During the months of February, March and April of that year 8,425 Italians arrived in Boston from Italy, and they are bound to continue coming at that high rate.[29]

Nevertheless, the year 1904 brought with it a ray of hope for the plight of the Italian people for Giovanni Giolitti,[30] the most prominent Italian statesman since Cavour, became premier.

The decade 1904 to 1914, often referred to as the Giolitti Decade or Era, was marked by the administration of the most enlightened of Italian statesmen in more than half a century. It is paradoxical, however, that it was also the greatest decade of Italian mass migration. Giolitti's prime concern was the reestablishment of democratic policies. He hoped to achieve them by widening the suffrage, and, most importantly, by introducing alienated Catholics, socialists, nationalists, and lower classes into Italian political life.

Building bridges with the myriad groups which were labelled "socialists"[31] was a particularly difficult undertaking. The Catholic Church has but one policymaker. The term "socialist," on the other hand, was used to describe the disenchanted masses we currently identify as Marxists, anarchists, national socialists, democratic socialists, and many other varieties. Giolitti's policy was to appeal to the center of the socialist faction by getting social legislation passed which, he hoped, would keep this element within the framework of the existing government. His government nationalized the railroads in 1905. Ports and harbors were modernized. By 1910, the Italian merchant marine had become one of the largest in Europe. Labor unions were allowed to merge to form the Italian General Confederation of Labor in 1906. That same year, a labor council was established to act as intermediary between labor and government. Construction trades were stimulated by the erection of a great number of public buildings throughout the country, with special emphasis again being placed north of the *Mezzogiorno*. From 1900 to 1914, the number of industrial enterprises increased from 117,000 to 224,000. In the ten years Giolitti was premier, foreign trade doubled. During that same period, agricultural output also doubled. This meant more work and higher taxes for the South, and higher profits for the North. Illiteracy was cut in half nationally,[32] but in Avellino, the literacy rate remained appallingly low. In fact, more than 50 percent of the population of the *Mezzogiorno* remained illiterate by 1914. There was close to a 100 percent increase in the miles of railroad track laid north of Rome. To the South, however, the government position was that the earthquake rate made it almost impossible significantly to increase rail service there. In the Province of Avellino, from which most of the North End Italians came, citizens were virtually cut off from the remainder of the peninsula until the Mussolini government built a major highway through the province in the early 1930s.[33]

Much of Giolitti's success could be attributed to the ever-increasing Italian emigration, which began during the Crispi regime, and which Giolitti did very little to halt. In fact, North End Italian immigration increased significantly during the Giolitti decade when the Italian population of the North End of Boston grew from 20,000 to more than 33,000. The causes of this dramatic increase become apparent when one observes that Giolitti's greatest social failures came in his policies towards the *Mezzogiorno*. Basically, he felt that centuries of neglect could not be eliminated overnight. His gradualist policies eventually led to inaction. Since it was not until 1912 that land ownership and literacy were dropped as voting requirements, it is little wonder that the *contadini* did not have a voice in their government. The members of the Chamber of Deputies, for example, who represented Avellino until this time were primarily absentee land owners who lived in the North. As taxes in Campania, Abruzzi, and Sicily continued to escalate beyond the means of the *contadini*, tenant farmers were forced into the position of day-laborers in increasing numbers. The cycle of poverty continued unabated for the southern peasant class, while the dramatic economic improvements of the period were directed primarily to the North, which was home to most of the policy-makers. Emigration began to look very inviting to millions of *contadini* who could no longer support their precious families.

Natural disasters also played a significant role in the Italian emigration decision. In 1905, a series of earthquakes hit the Provinces of Calabria and Basilicata. As many as thirty thousand were killed. In the following year,

Mount Vesuvius erupted, burying entire towns near Naples, reminiscent of the destruction of Pompeii nearly two thousand years earlier. The Naples area, a part of Campania, had already suffered famine, drought, and cholera within the lifetime of these residents. The significant increase in immigration to the North End of Boston from Campania during this decade must be attributed to the government's neglect and the region's continued natural disasters.

Sicily, and its province of Messina in particular, was the other region heavily represented in the North End's population. In 1908, one of the worst disasters of the century befell Messina. An earthquake so horrendous took place that over 100,000 people were killed. An additional 20,000 suffered a similar fate across the Straits of Messina in Reggio di Calabria. Ninety percent of the city of Messina was destroyed. In 1910, Sicily suffered another calamity, with Mount Etna erupting and killing about 10,000 people.

The violence of the Crispi era was replaced by the government's neglect of the South during the Giolittian decade. This failure to solve the "problem of the *Mezzogiorno*," coupled with the worst disasters nature could inflict, caused millions of *contadini* to decide *campanilismo* must be sacrificed for the preservation of *la famiglia*. In 1913 alone, almost one half million southern Italians emigrated to North and South America. Immigrants from Avellino, Naples, Messina, Palermo, Salerno, and many other communities of the *Mezzogiorno*, came to Boston to escape famine, earthquake, and repressive political policies which made life in Italy increasingly less desirable. They were also searching for economic betterment. The strength of the family structure, and a sense of identity molded by the values of *la via vecchia* made this transition possible.

2

Enclaves and New Villages

The Italians who moved to Boston at the turn of the century settled in a neighborhood which had experienced decades of decay. The North End, which boasted some of the most impressive residences in North America prior to the American Revolution, experienced a significant physical deterioration during the nineteenth century. By 1880, this once proud neighborhood of English gardens, Wren-like churches, Georgian mansions, and proper Bostonians, only remotely resembled the neighborhood Thomas Hutchinson once proudly called home. The end of the Revolution brought about a demographic shift; affluent loyalists did not return to their North End residences, and wealthy supporters left the community to take up desirable Beacon Hill addresses, at least in part because as Boston grew, they found the North End too close to the docks and commercial section of the city. By 1800, many North End mansions, large and stately as they were, lay vacant for want of individuals of adequate means. This inexorable outward rippling of established Boston families created a vacuum which new immigrants would fill. Individual rooms in North End mansions soon became home to entire families. Whatever space the local poor did not take was quickly occupied by newly arrived German and then Irish immigrants. Indigent and uneducated, these newest members of the community hastened the deterioration process by bringing with them little sense of urban hygiene. Sanitation was non-existent. Disease, which had not been a stranger to the North End even in more affluent times, became so widespread that, by 1845, the North End suffered a communicable disease rate twice that of the remainder of the city.

So significant was the deterioration of the neighborhood that by the 1840s the North End was Boston's first tenement slum. Paula Todisco, in a monograph for the general reader concerning the North End—*Boston's First Neighborhood,*—graphically describes the destitute Irish masses that inhabited this section of the city after the great potato famine of 1846:

> Poor, desperate, starving, they began to crowd into the North End and Fort Hill sections of Boston, searching for any means to sustain existence. They took the lowest, meanest jobs in Boston in order to subsist. . . . All through the North End the unfortunate Irish huddled.

Overcrowded, undernourished, they were incongruous inhabitants of the once fine houses of the fashionable. . . . As foreigners they were alternately tolerated and distrusted, victims of economic conditions over which they had no control. By 1850 they made up half of the North End population of 23,000. In 1855, 14,000 out of 26,000 North Enders were Irish born. The number of Irish peaked around 1880, and then rapidly dropped off in the face of new immigrant waves. But it was a miserable fifty years they spent here.[1]

The Italian masses that followed the Irish into the North End shared much in common. Though not as beset upon as the Irish, these new immigrants were indeed among the poorest of Boston's new citizens. Like the Irish, the Italians would be condemned for a lack of cleanliness, customs that bordered on the barbarous, and a religious faith that had not yet become acceptable to American society as a whole. The human discomfort of the Irish years increased during the Italian occupancy of the North End. So great did the overcrowding and its concomitant misery become, that the North End rivaled Calcutta, India, in density of population by 1900.[2]

It is not sufficient to identify these North End Italian residents as a homogeneous group, as the United States government did in its census and immigration studies. The true depths of North End Italian frustration cannot adequately be appreciated unless regional differences are taken into consideration. It subsequently becomes very important to arrive at more exact demographic statistics for the North End during the entire period of Italian settlement there. Existing data often appear to be sufficient, but, because of this perceptual inability of census takers to appreciate the importance of Italian subcultures, arriving at exact demographic statistics becomes a frustrating task. Though the Massachusetts census of 1905 and the United States census materials of 1890-1930 provide valuable, and, for the most part, reliable information, for a variety of reasons these statistics tend to be quite conservative. A basic mistrust of government[3] in general caused many Italians to give improper information. They often avoided census takers altogether, in the hope of preventing the deportation of relatives and *paesani* living illegally in the neighborhood.[4] In other instances, as stated by octogenarian Anthony Poto,[5] whose family was actively involved in the "Padrone System"[6] in Boston, immigrant families purposely misled the census takers, fearing that a full disclosure may have resulted in higher rents. More than one family often shared the same apartment. There were also many seasonal residents of the community whose numbers would not necessarily appear on any census data. Seasonal residents were individuals who worked in the United States during the spring and summer months, and returned to the warmer climate and relatives in Italy during the fall. Recent research[7] has shown that this practice was more widespread than hitherto had been believed. Further to complicate the researcher's task, Italian language newspapers and literature[8] of all sorts, written by trusted *paesani,* often give very high density statistics, in comparison to English language sources.

Plate 1. A view of Fleet Street in 1878. These structures were
typical of the deteriorated housing facilities the earliest
Genoese residents of the North End inherited from the
Irish. Courtesy of the Bostonian Society.

Plate 2. A typical Sunday morning scene in front of Sacred Heart Church (to right of photo) in North Square. Photo was taken in 1889, the year the church was officially opened for Catholic service. Courtesy of the Bostonian Society.

Plate 3. Children playing in front of the Paul Revere House in 1890 when it was an Avellinese tenement. The house was restored in 1906. Courtesy of the Bostonian Society.

Plate 4.   Merchants at the Salem Street store of Martignetti
Brothers in 1927. This firm was one of the most popular
Avellinese food import houses in Boston. Note the Pastene
label; by this time Pastene had become a wholesale
distributor. Courtesy of the Bostonian Society.

Another statistical consideration which must be dealt with here is that the North End was—and is—the center of Italian life in the Boston area.[9] Italians who moved to East Boston, Charlestown, the West End, or South Boston, returned to the North End for all religious functions and weekly shopping. They would even be provided bed and/or board in their parents' and relatives' apartments whenever needed. This type of transient population, which would not appear on any census data, regularly swelled the neighborhood's already overcrowded streets.

It must be stressed at the outset that we are examining slightly less than 100 acres of land when we discuss the North End of Boston (see map 4). Of this tract, only 70 acres traditionally have been used for housing. The remaining 30 acres make up the waterfront area, which virtually surrounds that section of the city. By comparison, the parking lot at Florida's Disneyworld is three times larger than the inhabited area of the North End.

The North End, as small as it is, has always been a community of neighborhoods. Persons were and are identified as being lifelong residents of "North Street," "near Saint Mary's," "lower Prince Street," "down on Salem Street." These and other such designations not only identify a section of the North End but usually tell the part of Italy from which a family came, which church it frequents, what its social status is, and what "clubs" its members belong to. From the Italian community's earliest days in the North End these designations were determined by "regional enclaves."

The first such "enclave" grew out of the arrival of the Genoese immigrants who settled on Ferry Court in the 1860s. Map 5 shows the locations of North End ethnic groups. Ferry Court does not exist today, but was located adjacent to North Street, near the Fulton Street poultry slaughter house district of the city. Of the 26,000 residents of the North End then, about 14,000 were Irish (see figure 2). The remainder were mostly of Anglo-Saxon background,[10] some of whom were from Nova Scotia. The Ferry Court community numbered fewer than 200 Italians, accounting for 8 percent of the total Italian population of Massachusetts in 1860. "Southern Italians, and especially Sicilians," one contemporary chronicler notes,[11] "constituted a minority." It is important to keep this observation in mind because as the Italian population of the community grew, the regions of Italy specifically represented changed.

The Genoese residents made their living as fruit, wine, cheese, and olive oil merchants to the Italian community of Greater Boston. Two of the most prominent Genoese in the North End at this time were Pietro Pastene and Alessandro Badaracco. In 1874, Pietro Pastene opened his first food shop, on 229 Hanover Street, specializing in Italian products. In 1880, he moved his business to 87 Fulton Street, in the heart of the Genoese district. By 1901, his business expanded to the point that it was able to utilize all the space from 69 to 75 Fulton Street. Today, the New York-based Pastene Corporation is a major food importer. Allesandro Badaracco, on the other hand, was one of the earliest Italian immigrants in the North End. Badaracco, who settled in the North End prior to the Civil War, ran the largest fruit business in Boston by the late nineteenth century.[12] It must be noted, however, that the success of both Pastene and Badaracco was not representative of all the Genoese of the day, for the vast majority were owners of much smaller establishments.

The 1880 population of the North End was slightly less than the 26,000 figure of 1860.[13] As figure 2 shows, the Irish numbered almost 16,000, and much of the balance was made up mostly of Anglo-Saxons. The Jewish, Italian, and Portuguese population accounted for about four thousand. Leveroni, Bushee, and Woods[14] all agree that the Italian population of the North End was slightly less than one thousand of that four thousand.

During the two decades from 1860 to 1880 the Ferry Court community spilled over into two neighboring streets in the poultry district, so that the Ferry Court-North Street-Fulton Street triangle became home to these newcomers.[15] (See map 5.)

During that same period, a few Genoese moved into North Bennett Street, pushing out mainly Irish residents. In 1873, the Italian-Portuguese Catholic Church of Saint John the Baptist was dedicated there. By then, marked dissension began to surface between the Genoese, who now inhabited Ferry Court and parts of North Bennett Street, and the more recent Campanian immigrants who lived on North Square. This North-South friction would characterize the neighborhood's social, religious, and economic life throughout the entire period.

The 1880s was a critical decade for the immigrant community of the North End because ever-increasing taxes, natural disasters, and unfavorable government policies in Italy, as well as pogroms in Russia,[16] drastically altered the ethnic makeup of the North End.[17] By 1895, the total population of the North End was approximately 23,800. (See figure 1.) The decrease of about two thousand from 1880 was primarily due to the physical deterioration of the neighborhood and the accessibility of three of Boston's newest communities: Roxbury, West Roxbury, and Dorchester. The Metropolitan Street Railway Company and the subsequent West End Street Railway Company made it possible for those communities to increase in population from 60,000 in 1870 to 227,000 in 1900.[18] Of the 23,800 residents of the North End, the Italians now numbered 7,700. (See figure 2.) Though this did not represent a majority, it was clearly the largest single ethnic group in the North End. While the once dominant Irish population still numbered 6,800, their numbers represented a decrease of nearly 10,000 in 15 years. The Jewish population, on the other hand, had increased from 3,500 in 1880 to 6,200 in 1895. There were 1,200 Anglo-Saxons, and 800 Portuguese residents of the community as well.

The Italian community naturally outgrew the confines of the Ferry Court area and North Bennett Street by 1895, expanding to include the area bound by Prince Street-Salem Street-Tileston Street-Hanover Street, and also much of the area bound by Hanover Street-North Square-Fulton Street. (See map 6.)

The first area mentioned became home to the Italian community from Abruzzi, and some Neapolitans.[19] The Genoese community continued to inhabit North Bennett Street and North Bennett Court. The remainder of Salem Street, and its adjoining courts, was home to the ever-increasing Jewish community in the North End. (See map 6.) There were two Jewish synagogues located in this section, Beth Abraham on Salem Street, and Beth Israel on Baldwin Place.

The second section mentioned was now inhabited by Campanians from towns such as Taurasi, Chiusano San Domenico, and Mirabella Eclano in the Province of Avellino. This province, a very distinct 30 miles from Naples by provincial Italian standards,[20] provided the North End with the greatest number of immigrants of all the Italian provinces.

It is important to note this here because there has long been a popular misconception that Sicily provided the community with the greatest number of immigrants. The Sacramental Records of both Italian churches in the North End clearly show that from 1873 to 1930, the province of Avellino (see map 3) in Campania was the most often represented place of birth by a wide margin. This fact will be carefully analyzed in the next chapter.

From 1870 to 1895, the growth of the Italian community in the North End closely resembled Italian immigration to the United States. (See figure 3.) The numbers were relatively few, and the regions represented were scattered throughout the Italian peninsula, with some immigrants coming from Sicily as well. As figure 4 shows, by the turn of the century, both Italian immigration to the United States and the size of the Italian colony in the North End increased dramatically. Most of the new immigrants in both cases came from the Regions of Campania and Sicily. More than one hundred thousand Italians entered the United States in 1901. The annual number of Italian immigrants entering the United States would not drop below that figure until World War I in 1914. From 1905 to 1907 alone, close to one million Italian immigrants entered the United States. The single greatest year for Italian immigration to the United States was 1913, with 376,776 entering the country.

The twenty years from 1900 to 1920 witnessed an increase in the Italian population of Boston, from 18,000 to 77,000 (see figures 5 and 6), representing a growth from 2 percent to over 10 percent of the total Boston population by 1920. The North End Italian population during that same time period increased from 14,000 to 37,000 (see figure 2), an increase from 60 percent to over 95 percent of the North End population. Most of the Irish and Jewish population of the North End had moved "up" to Roxbury, Dorchester, and Hyde Park, by then. The Italians spread well beyond the "enclaves" they had initially established for themselves in 1860. The significant Sicilian population, which settled in the community after 1900 (see maps 7 and 8), occupied the length of North Street, with heaviest concentrations in the Fleet Street section of North Street. Both of the streets adjoined the fish pier area, which the Sicilians utilized more than other Italian groups. This area also became home for the Calabrians, with their heaviest concentration farther down on North Street in the Commercial Street area.

The community from the Province of Avellino continued to increase in size after 1900, by this time inhabiting the Shaefe Street-Copps Hill area of the North End, as well as North Square. The Genoese community of North Bennett Street and Fulton Street did not grow to any extent after 1900 (see map 7). Some moved to Charlestown, just over the City Square Bridge. They continued to return to the North End by foot and the new elevated rail line, for all their social and religious activities. The Genoese and other Northern Italian immigrants who left the community because they felt uncomfortable living in a now predominantly southern Italian neighborhood were not replaced by other northern Italians. Most northern Italian emigration was directed to South America after 1900,[21] partially due to new trans-Atlantic shipping routes and the receptivity of South American countries such as Argentina and Brazil to Italian immigrants. At a time when the lure of free or inexpensive farm land ceased in the United States, Argentina offered Italian farmers prime farm land at giveaway prices. Similar incentives were available in Brazil. Northern Italians were better able to make a minimal investment such as this, and pay the additional ship's passage, than the *contadini* from the South.

In terms of subcultural neighborhoods, the North End resembled the Italian countryside by 1920. A community which had once been home to a variety of nationalities became home to a cross section of Italian subcultures. Their enclaves were created intentionally to assert the importance and security of *la via vecchia*. By the creation of these new villages, the old world of *campanilismo* had been brought to Boston.

Map 4. City of Boston, 1915

(CAMBRIDGE)

Charlestown

East
Boston

West
End

NORTH
END

Brighton

South
End

South
Boston

Allston

Roxbury

(BROOKLINE)

Jamaica
Plain

West
Roxbury

Dorchester

Hyde
Park

Map 5. Major North End Ethnic Groups, 1880

Map 6. Major North End Ethnic Groups, 1895

CHARLES RIVER

NORTH PIER

SOUTH PIER

NORTH END BEACH

COMMERCIAL ST

COPPS HILL
BURIAL GROUND

CHARTER ST

PRINCE ST

HULL ST

SHEAFE ST

SALEM ST

UNKNOWN ST

BATTERY ST

CLARK ST

ENDICOTT ST

NORTH MARGIN ST

COOPER ST

HANOVER ST

FLEET ST

COMMERCIAL ST

NORTH SQ

RICHMOND ST

CROSS ST

NORTH ST

FULTON ST

FULTON ST

PORTUGUESE   AVELLINESI

JEWS   SICILIANI

IRISH   ABRUZZESI   } ITALIANS

GENOVESI

Map 7. Major North End Ethnic Groups, 1910

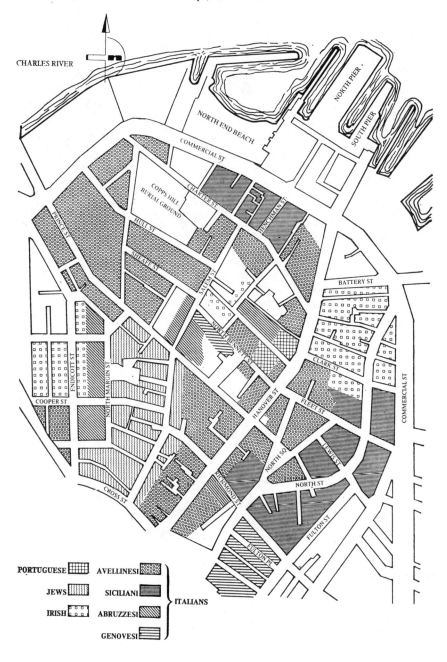

CHARLES RIVER

NORTH PIER

SOUTH PIER

NORTH END BEACH

COMMERCIAL ST

COPPS HILL
BURIAL GROUND

CHARTER ST

SHEAFE ST

HULL ST

PRINCE ST

SALEM ST

BATTERY ST

NORTH BENNET ST

FLEET ST

CLARK ST

ENDICOTT ST

NORTH MARGIN ST

COOPER ST

HANOVER ST

NORTH SQ

LEWIS ST

COMMERCIAL ST

RICHMOND ST

NORTH ST

CROSS ST

FULTON PL

FULTON ST

PORTUGUESE AVELLINESI

JEWS SICILIANI   ITALIANS

IRISH ABRUZZESI

GENOVESI

Map 8. Major North End Ethnic Groups, 1925

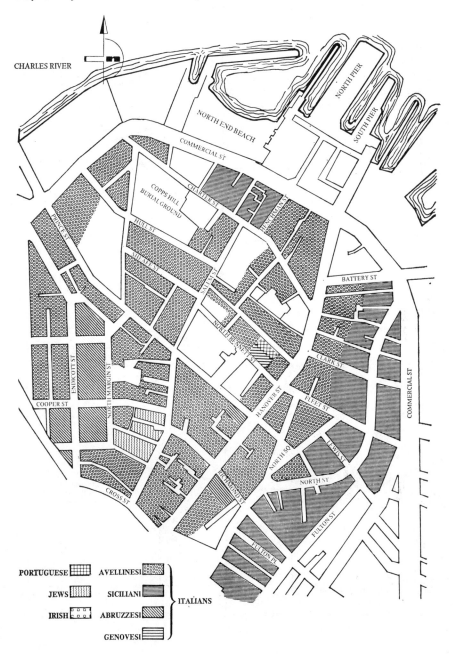

CHARLES RIVER

NORTH PIER

SOUTH PIER

NORTH END BEACH

COMMERCIAL ST

COPPS HILL
BURIAL GROUND

CHARTER ST

HULL ST

SNOW HILL ST

PRINCE ST

SHEAFE ST

SALEM ST

BATTERY ST

NORTH BENNET ST

CLARK ST

ENDICOTT ST

NORTH MARGIN ST

HANOVER ST

FLEET ST

COOPER ST

CLARK ST

COMMERCIAL ST

RICHMOND ST

NORTH SQ

TILESTON ST

NORTH ST

CROSS ST

FULTON PL

FULTON ST

PORTUGUESE   AVELLINESI

JEWS   SICILIANI   } ITALIANS

IRISH   ABRUZZESI

GENOVESI

Figure 1. Population of City of Boston and principal foreign-born groups in Boston (left scale); population of the North End of Boston, 1870-1930 (right scale) *(in Thousands)*

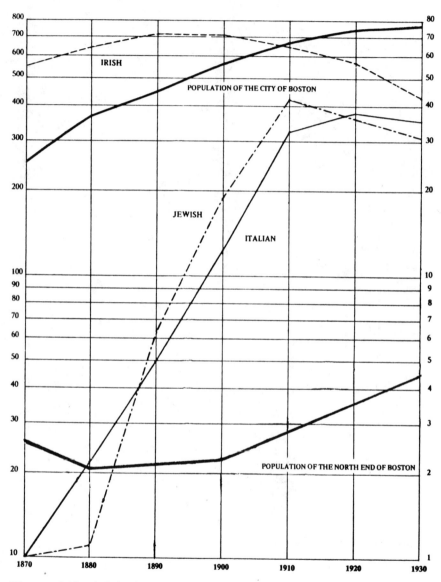

IRISH

POPULATION OF THE CITY OF BOSTON

JEWISH

ITALIAN

POPULATION OF THE NORTH END OF BOSTON

*Figures compiled from the Registry Department of the City of Boston, 1870-1900; Boston Statistics, 1900-1930.

Figure 2.   Foreign Population (Including Second Generation) of
North End of Boston, 1870-1930 *(in Thousands)*

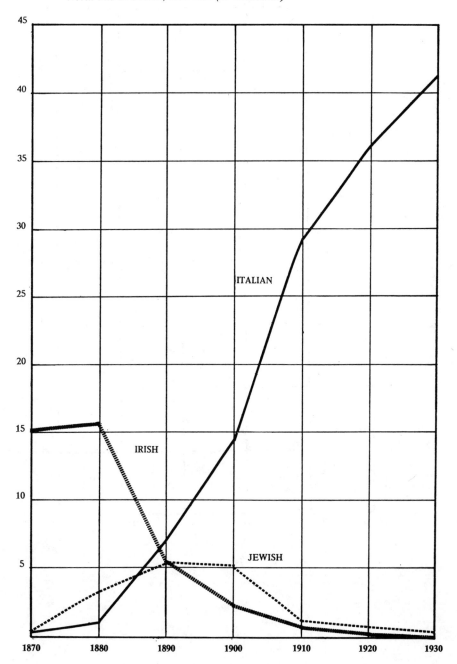

Figure 3. Total Italian Immigration to the United States, 1870-1895

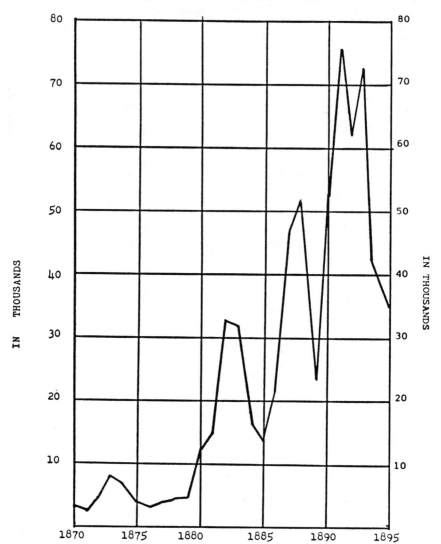

Figure 4. Total Italian Immigration to the United States, 1895-1930

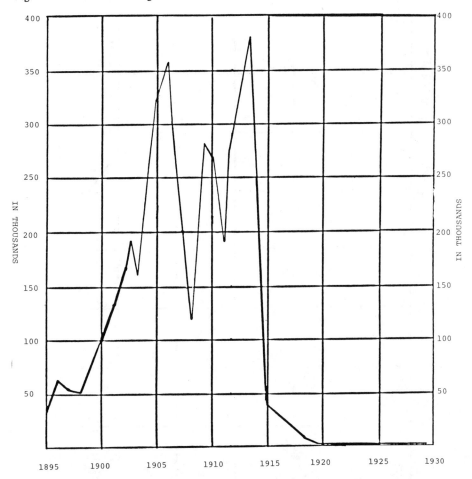

Figure 5. Principal Foreign-Born Groups in Boston, 1870-1930

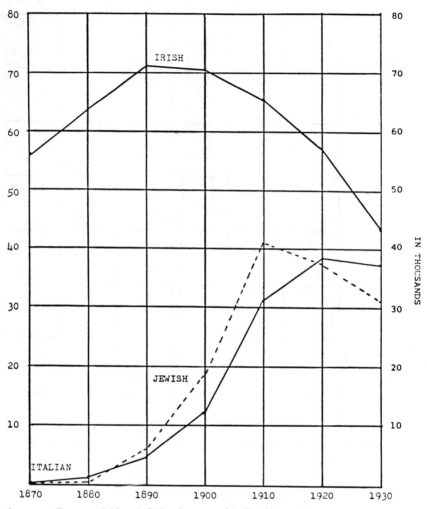

Source: Figures compiled from the Registry Department of the City of Boston, 1870-
1900; Boston Statistics, 1900-1930.

3

New World Enclave—Old World Marriage

One of the reasons we know so little about the Italian "enclaves" of the North End is that hitherto too much credence was given to the Dillingham Commission Report, which failed adequately to identify and analyze them. The "enclaves" discussed in the previous chapter were indeed an important element in the life of the North End Italian community. An examination of the 1910 *United States Senate Report of the Immigration Commission,* more popularly identified as the "Dillingham Commission Report,"[1] raises more questions about the existence of the enclaves than it resolves. For example, while the report identified Campania, Sicily, and Abruzzi as the three Italian regions most often represented in the North End, it did not describe whether individuals from each of these three Italian regions tended to group according to "regions of origin" when searching for housing. Nor did it adequately compare numbers of individuals from each of these three regions. The report also failed to describe which provinces within the three regions identified were most often represented. This becomes particularly important when attempting to establish whether "chain emigration patterns" (recent immigrants encouraging relatives and friends to join them) existed.

Since the Dillingham Commission Report had been so highly regarded for its demographic profiles, any attempt at a demographic study of the North End at the turn of the century should begin with an analysis of volumes 26 and 27 of the 1910 *United States Senate Report of the Immigration Commission.* This 42-volume work studied the impact of immigration on American society. Both the report itself, and the manner in which it was used, have been widely criticized[2] for lack of objectivity, and the undue influence immigration restriction organizations had with the members of the committee. Nonetheless, it does provide a glimpse, albeit jaded, of immigrant life in 1910 America, which I intend to change and update in this study.

A brief reexamination of the applicable sections of the Dillingham Report is required here, because it provides one view of the neighborhood under study.

Volumes 26 and 27, entitled "Immigrants in Cities," presented an analysis of the immigrant population of seven cities. Generalizations about the immigrant population of New York, Chicago, Philadelphia, Boston, Cleveland, Buffalo, and Milwaukee were made, based on selective neighborhood samplings. Seven areas in Boston, designated "districts," were analyzed in 132 pages. The report failed to mention why these Boston "districts" were chosen, other than the obvious fact that they contained an immigrant population. These "districts" were located in Boston's West End, North End, and South End, as well as South Boston and Dorchester.

Though the introduction of the Boston report presented interesting descriptions about the two North End "districts" studied, 133 of the 140 charts included in the Boston report contain only composite information of all seven Boston "districts" presented. It is thus not possible to determine exact information about the North End from these charts alone.

The entire Boston study included a sampling of 326 South Italian and 15 North Italian "households," representing a total of 1,799 persons in all of Boston. The two North End "districts" analyzed in the report included 278 South Italian and 12 North Italian "households," totaling 1,487 individuals. The North End thus represented 85.7 percent of all Italians in the Boston survey, a percentage that will be employed every time the Dillingham Report presents cumulative citywide data. This will help to approximate North End Italians statistics.

Two of the seven Boston "districts" studied in the North End, were designated the "Hanover Street District" and "Morton Street District." A careful study of both of these "districts" will assist in identifying the social makeup of the North End. It will also point to the accuracy of the Italian sections of the report because the non-Italian findings are verifiable through other sources.

The "Hanover Street District" was made up of the two blocks bounded by Hanover, Commercial, Charter, and Henchman Streets. There were 308 households in this "district," only eleven of which were listed as "native-born households" (general nativity of head of household). Interestingly, the report labeled three of these eleven heads of household as belonging to the "White Race." The remaining eight were distributed in the following manner: one English, one German, four Irish, and *South Italian* (italics mine). A distinction was made in all 42 volumes between South Italians and North Italians under the category of race. This was in keeping with my findings[3] about the Italian perception of their own racial identity at the time. Of the 297 families with foreign-born heads of household, 260 were South Italian and 10 were North Italian. The remaining 27 heads of household were: 10 Irish, 4 Canadian (non-French), 4 Norwegian, 3 Swedish, 2 Portuguese, 2 Greek, 1 Spanish, and 1 Russian Hebrew. Though the Irish, Canadian (Nova Scotian),

Portuguese, and Jewish presence has been already mentioned, the Swedish, Norwegian, and Greek residence in these two blocks came as somewhat of a surprise. The report failed to shed light on why these groups resided in the North End. Oral testimony showed the existence of an occasional Greek family in the North End.[4]

The other North End "district" analyzed by the report, called the "Morton Street District," was bounded by Morton, Wiget, Cross, and North Margin Streets, which the Dillingham Commission called the "Polish District."[5] The report called these "Poles" Russian Jews. The Dillingham Commission, which misrepresented North End Italians, also gave misleading information concerning Lithuanians and non-Jewish Poles.[6] While most of the North End Lithuanians were Catholics, the commission only identified the Poles as having non-Jews among their population. As they did with their Italian statistics, the Dillingham Commission barely scratched the surface in their appraisal of the neighborhood here. I had hoped that the commission's findings in Boston would have been helpful not only in my attempt to arrive at a composite image of the North End, but, more importantly, the Italian subcultures represented there. While the composite image of the North End proved to be merely adequate at best, their data concerning Italians were often incorrect altogether.

The commission was mistaken from the outset when it identified Italian regions as Italian provinces. It then proceeded to list Rome as a province in southern Italy.[7] Romans, who, like Bostonians, feel they are at the hub of the civilized world, would certainly take umbrage with such a designation. The commission analyzed the "Italian Province of Birth" of the "head of household"[8] for all seven Boston "districts." Of the 270 North End Italian households sampled, 110 were "headed" by Campanians (40.7 percent), 74 by Sicilians (27.4 percent), and 36 by Abruzzesi (13.3 percent). My research, based primarily upon oral testimony and archival material to this point, made me feel that while the Campanian figure may have been accurate, the Sicilian and Abruzzese figures were certainly too high. I kept remembering the comments of the Abruzzese Luisa Digiustini, who said:

> You know, there never were really that many of my *paesani* here. Sure, we lived together near Saint Mary's and a few other areas, but this was the neighborhood of Avellinesi.

The statistics of the Dillingham Commission had to be analyzed and verified.

One of the most interesting ways of checking "head of household" statistics is to study marriage records. This is valuable not only because it will validate or invalidate earlier findings, but also because studies show that Italians had a relatively high intramarriage rate.[9] If a high intramarriage rate existed among North End Italians, then we would not only test the validity of the "enclave theory" as such, but also show that *la via vecchia* (old world values), as described in chapter 1, truly existed in the North End during this time. Consequently, a study of Italian marriage records in the North End would aid in proving: (1) the Dillingham Commission Report to be inadequate in its description of North End Italian subcultures, (2) Italians in general, and Southern Italians in particular, retained strong provincial loyalties in Boston, and (3) the precise origin of these North End Italians.

The marriage records of Saint Leonard's Church[10] on Prince Street and Sacred Heart Church on North Square, Italian churches just one short block apart, show that from 1873 to 1929, 36,616 individuals were married. The great number of weddings involved was one reason a total study was considered unmanageable. There were other difficulties as well. From 1873 to 1908 (see table 1), Saint Leonard's Church failed to record the "Place of Birth" in their Sacramental Files. Thereafter, no regular pattern of recording was followed, with the village being listed in some instances, and only the province or region cited in others. This required a study of the location of some of the smaller Italian villages. Sacred Heart Church, on the other hand, did keep complete marriage records from 1890 onward. Their Sacramental Files began late in 1889. In this instance as well "the place of birth" designation contained village, provincial, *or* regional notation, but rarely all three.

Intramarriage between individuals of the same province, intramarriage between southern Italians of different regions, intermarriage between northern and southern Italians, and marriage with non-Italians was also noted. Listing Italian second generation intermarriage posed a problem because all that is listed in the Sacramental Files is the "place of birth." When an American place of birth is cited with an Italian surname, it was assumed that they were second generation Italian, though, in fact, they may have been third or even fourth generation. Four sample years, 1899, 1909, 1919, and 1929 were chosen. It was decided that if there was any significant variance in any of the categories, additional years would have to be investigated. The four years studied involved a sample of 3,164 individuals, or 8.07 percent[11] of all weddings in the two churches from 1873 to 1929. Of this total, 164 individuals are included only in the total number of weddings, and no other category, because 164 was the number of individuals married in Saint Leonard's Church in 1899, a year in which their Sacramental Files failed to cite any "place of birth."

It should be noted at the outset that Italians generally married other Italians of the same generation. Only 7 percent of the total number of weddings sampled were between Italians of different generations. Tillie Sablone,[12] herself a second generation Italian, gave an interesting explanation for this when she described her marriage to Jimmy Sablone, an immigrant from Abruzzi:

Table 1. Number of North End Marriages by Church and Year

	Year	Total Number of Marriages	Total Province Intramarriage		Total Region Intramarriage		Marriages by South Itals. of Different Regions	Total North-South Italian Intermar.		Total Ital. 2nd Gen. Intermarriage		Total Ital. Non-Ital. Intermarriage	
Sacred Heart	1899	141	118	83.6%	127	90%	7	4.9%	0	0	3	2.1%	3	2.1%
Saint Leonard	1899	82	These records were not kept from 1873-1908.											
Sacred Heart	1909	389	329	84.5%	341	87.6%	14	3.5%	4	1.0%	17	4.3%	3	.77%
Saint Leonard	1909	180	142	78.8%	156	86.6%	5	2.7%	1	.5%	12	6.6%	6	3.3%
Sacred Heart	1919	351	268	76.3%	298	84.9%	13	3.7%	0	0	38	10.8%	2	.56%
Saint Leonard	1919	167	135	80.8%	141	84.4%	8	4.7%	1	.59%	16	9.5%	0	0
Sacred Heart	1929	160	141	88.1%	144	90%	2	1.2%	0	0	10	6.2%	4	2.5%
Saint Leonard	1929	112	98	88.4%	100	89.2%	3	2.6%	0	0	9	8%	0	0
TOTALS		1,582	1231	82%	1307	87.1%	52	3.4%	6	4%	105	7%	18	1.2%

Many Italian parents wanted their children to marry "Americans." Of course they meant Italians who were born here. Especially in the case of daughters, parents were very protective, and did not trust recent male immigrants. Some of them may have had wives or sweethearts in the old country, and were just looking for some fun. I married Jimmy because he was so handsome, and my family loved him as much as I did. That was the exception, though. Jimmy's family in Italy knew my parents, anyway.

Of the total nunber of weddings studied, an astonishing cumulative average of 82.0 percent were between individuals from the same Italian province—people from Avellino, for example, married other people from Avellino 82.0 percent of the time. Most of the marriages in this category were between individuals from the same village or town. Most of those interviewed did not find this surprising, for, as Tillie Sablone commented: "What could be more natural? They had everything in common."

Observing this category by decades proved to be very interesting. In 1899, 83.6 percent of the marriages in Sacred Heart Church were between individuals from the same province. As expected, the 1909 statistic was similar, with 84.5 percent in the same category. Ten years later, however, a drop of 8.2 percent was noted, with 76.3 percent of all marriages being between individuals from the same province. This may have been caused by the negligible Italian immigration during World War I, which limited the number of eligible Italians for marriage. This downward trend was dramatically reversed ten years later, with 1929 recording 88.1 percent, which was the highest provincial intramarriage rate of all.

The statistics for Saint Leonard's Church were similar in this category. In 1909, 78.8 percent of those married were from the same Italian province. In 1919, that percentage went to 80.8 percent, and it jumped to 88.4 percent ten years later. Interestingly, both Sacred Heart and Saint Leonard Churches had identical 88 percent averages in the "same province intramarriage" category in 1929.

There is one other point to be made here. Even though the 26 southern Italian provinces, shown in map 3, where generally mentioned with the same frequency in both churches,[13] different towns within those provinces were mentioned in each church. More than 60 percent of those weddings were between individuals from the same town. Consequently, the towns of Taurasi (see map 3), Chiusano San Domenico, and Mirabella Eclano, all in the province of Avellino, were the most represented towns overall. While the first two dominated Sacred Heart's files, they were only occasionally mentioned in the Saint Leonard's records, where Mirabella Eclano was more frequent an entry. The Sicilian town of Sciacca, in the province of Girgenti, was mentioned 14 times in the Sacred Heart files, but mentioned only once in the Saint Leonard's records. In this case, the Sciacca weddings were all intramarriages within the same town.

Based on the oral testimony I gathered for this study, not all of these marriages of individuals from the same province were blessed by *la famiglia* from the start. One octogenarian couple, who requested that their identity be kept confidential, told a heart-wrenching story:

> We were cousins living in the same town in Sicily when we fell in love more than sixty years ago. Our families were, of course, totally against our getting married because we were cousins. We decided to escape to the United States. We had no money, so I had to work at odd jobs on farms until we could get to Naples. We came to Boston because I had a friend who had been writing to me for awhile, and he said that there was work here. During the next ten years we went back to Italy twice; our little daughter died on board ship on one of those voyages. We were still not accepted by our families. We did not return to Italy for another fifty years, and still there is hostility by those members of the family who are alive today. I have not seen most of my brothers and sisters all these years. More than half of them have died. I doubt if I will ever get to see my two brothers who live in Argentina.

The northern Italian provinces were presented more frequently in the Sacred Heart's Sacramental File, where intramarriage between northern Italians of the same province accounted for 4.1 percent of all the marriages in that church during the four sample years, and 7.4 percent of all marriages were between individuals of the same northern region. In the Saint Leonard Sacramental File, only 1.8 percent of the weddings recorded were between individuals of the same northern region. Again, different cities were mentioned. Ten couples from Como, fourteen from Milan, fifteen each from Piacenza and Genoa, and eight from Bologna were married in Sacred Heart Church. Saint Leonard showed no weddings involving individuals from Piacenza, Milan, Bologna, and Como. Only two weddings involved individuals from Genoa, and both of these were in 1909.

This variation of villages, towns, and cities represented in the respective Sacramental Files can be attributed to a retention of provincial ties just as the "enclaves" had demonstrated. As significant as this provincial intramarriage rate was, the percentage of intramarriage between individuals of the same region was even more dramatic.

Sacred Heart Church consistently maintained an 85 percent to 90 percent rate in this category of "regional intramarriage" during the four sample years. As was the case in the provincial intramarriage category, 1919 was the low year, with an 84.9 percent figure. Both 1899 and 1929 showed identical figures of 90 percent with 1909 recording 87.6 percent.

Saint Leonard's Sacramental File records showed almost identical figures, with 86.6 percent in 1909, 84.4 percent in 1919, and 89.2 percent in 1929. The cumulative rate of regional intramarriage for the four years sampled was 87.1 percent, or 2,614 out of a possible 3,000 individuals in both churches.

One of the more obvious characteristics of this category is that adjoining provinces had the highest intermarriage rate. Consequently, the "combination" of Avellino-Benevento (see map 3), and Naples-Caserta, all in Campania, appeared far more often than Salerno-Caserta, both at opposite extremes within the region. In the region of Sicily, Messina-Palermo and Catania-Siracusa were most common. These "combinations" were attributable to the strong sense of village and provincial loyalty which would be more willing to accept a "foreigner"[14] (*straniero*) from a nearby community than one from a greater distance.

The third category studied was the "intermarriage rate by southern Italians of different regions." Only 104 individuals out of the 3,000 sampled, or 3.4 percent, intermarried in this manner. Interestingly, the lowest statistic in this category was recorded in 1929. In both other categories thus far studied, this same year reflected a strengthening of traditional marriage patterns. The drop of 2.2 percent from 1919 to 1929 in this third category was more than offset by the dramatic rise in provincial and regional intramarriage during the same period. This drop also reflected a "return" to rather than a diminution of traditional marriage patterns.

The two regions with the greatest number of marriages in this category were Campania and Sicily. In both cases, however, two out of every three weddings were between individuals of adjoining regions. Avellino had the greatest number of such marriages with 16. The one province with the highest percentage of marriages outside its own region was Caltanisetta in Sicily (34 percent). All but one of the Caltanisetta marriages took place at Saint Leonard's Church.

Gaetano Grande[15] (see plate 20), whose 1906 marriage falls into this category of "intermarriage of southern Italians of Different Regions", reflected on the experience:

> I went to Naples from Siracusa, Sicily, in 1905, in search of work. I went to Avellino during the grape harvest season and met my wife. Because I was a Sicilian, I was not accepted by her family, so we decided to "run away" and get married. Of course, we couldn't go back, so we came to Boston, where we found more Avellinesi. Since I picked up my wife's dialect quickly, I decided to pass as Avellinese. This worked well. I opened a barber shop which attracted Neapolitans and Avellinesi. With a wife who cooked Avellinese-style, and my speaking the dialect at the shop, everyone thought I was from Avellino. I passed as Avellinese for almost thirty years, until a paesano from Siracusa arrived and told everyone I was a Sicilian. By that time I was accepted by the Avellinese, so it did not hurt my business. Twenty-five or thirty years earlier, who knows what would have happened!

This act of "passing" for a more desirable subcultural group was not unique to the Italians. It has long been a common practice among Blacks, and who knows how many other groups attempting to be accepted in a multicultural society.

Possibly the greatest indication of a continuation of the North-South Italian mistrust in Boston was the fact that only six northern Italians married southern Italians out of a total of 3,000 individuals sampled. This represented a mere .4 percent of the total number of marriages. No weddings of this sort took place in 1899 and 1929, the first and last years of this study, further indicating a return to traditional practices. In 1919, only one "mixed marriage"—this is certainly what it was considered by the community—took place, and it was at Saint Leonard's Church. In 1909, five couples exchanged vows, four of them at Sacred Heart and one at Saint Leonard. Four of the six weddings in the category involved Romans. Three of these Roman weddings were with Sicilians (2 Messina, 1 Caltanisetta), and one with a Campanian (Avellino). The three Rome-Sicily weddings were contrary to the tendency we observed of people marrying individuals from adjoining provinces or regions. The other two weddings in this category were between individuals from: (1) Savona, Liguria-Avellino, Campania, and (2) Vicenza, Veneto-Avellino, Campania. Again, these weddings did not follow the pattern we observed. The most logical explanation is that there are always exceptions to the norm, and, in this case, love probably conquered regional rivalries.

Only 18 Italians, or 1.2 percent married non-Italians during the four sample years. This rate was three times higher than the North-South Italian intermarriage rate. Nine of the weddings in this newest category were Italian-Irish. Of these, eight involved Italian men and Irish women. The remaining nine weddings involved two Swiss, and one French, Turkish, Austrian, German, Brazilian, Portuguese, and French Canadian respectively. Only one Swiss and the Brazilian had Italian surnames. Eleven of the Italians in this category were from northern Italy, four from southern Italy, and three were "second generation" Italian-Americans.

These marriage records indeed demonstrated the existence and continuance of Italian subcultural "enclaves," and further pointed to the inadequacy of the Dillingham Commission's Report. In spite of the fact the report's findings concerning Campanians (40.8 percent) and Sicilians (27.3 percent) were similar to the 1909 marriage records, there were more Campanians (42.3 percent) and fewer Sicilians (21.5 percent) in the neighborhood than the report indicated. A subtle, but important distinction must be made here. The Italian propensity for very close family ties, and an extremely high provincial intramarriage rate in Boston's North End suggests that certain buildings, or even blocks of buildings within the North End community, were mostly inhabited by individuals from the same Italian province, and, in many cases, the same village. (See maps 5-8). Thus, it was possible for the Dillingham Commission to arrive at a similar percentage for Campanians and Sicilians, but never properly to identify the province from which these individuals came. We can safely assume that the Campanians in the Dillingham study were not from the same province as Campanians living on North Square, for example, because of the "enclave theory."

In the case of other Italian subcultures, the latest findings were more dramatic. The Abbruzesi, for example, had only a 3.5 percent statistic in the marriage records, as compared to 13.2 percent in the Commission Report. The newer statistic is more in keeping with oral testimony described above. Calabrians were also far less represented in the marriage records (3 percent) than in the Commission Report (9.5 percent). The existence of "enclaves" probably explains the variance between the Dillingham Commission Report and Sacramental Files.

The study of North End marriage records illustrates the significance of Italian provincial loyalties in Boston. It shows that Italians in Boston consistently preferred marriage with individuals from their own province or region. They usually married individuals from a place as close to their old-world village as possible. Though both churches had a cross-section of southern Italian provinces and regions, different towns within those provinces were represented in each church. Northern Italians were represented in Sacred Heart's Sacramental Files at a much higher rate than at Saint Leonard's. Northern Italians married non-Italians at a higher rate than they married southern Italians. These practices remained relatively constant throughout the period studied, with old-world loyalties being the same or stronger in 1929 than in 1899.

Italian marriages in the North End secured the perpetuation of *la via vecchia* in much the same manner as their housing patterns. The importance of *la famiglia,* with its intricate network of relationships, was again asserted through the remarkable cohesion of the Italian subcultural community.

My research thus shows that the Dillingham Commission Report, while of some value, failed adequately to identify who these North End Italians really were, and just how significant were their old-world values.

4

Same Religion but Different Church

The existence of subcultural enclaves from the earliest days of the Italian settlement of the North End and the retention of *la via vecchia* (old world values) as exhibited in their marriage patterns were but two of the manifestations of the importance of Italian provincial loyalties. The religious practices of these sons and daughters of the *Mezzogiorno* equally represented their determined effort to retain ties which extended all the way to the villages of southern Italy.

The vast majority of Italian immigrants to Boston were Roman Catholics. Thus, it is not surprising that their earliest religious experiences were influenced by the Catholic Church. However, there is some controversy concerning the type of Catholics they were. Silvano Tomasi,[1] an authority on the religious practices of Italian-American Catholics, contends that the majority of them were Catholic by conviction as well as custom, both in Italy and in the United States. He feels that in this country national parishes, such as Sacred Heart Italian Church in North Square and Saint Leonard Church on Prince Street, were made necessary by the negative experiences Italians encountered in Irish Catholic Churches, and that these national parishes greatly aided in the Americanization process. On the other hand , Professor Rudolph Vecoli,[2] who has written widely concerning the peasant class of the *Mezzogiorno,* maintains that Italians were Catholics simply by custom. He agrees that national parishes grew in response to negative experiences Italians encountered in Irish Catholic churches, but he expresses grave doubts that these national parishes had any success in the Americanization process. It is my objective in this chapter to show that the earliest North End residents from the villages of Southern Italy experienced religious friction initially at the hands of their Irish coreligionists, and later among themselves.

The Catholic Church in Boston, though substantively the same as that in the old world *paese* (village), encouraged external religious practices which were basically Celtic rather than Italian.[3] The reluctance of both the local clergy and the Irish Catholic population to accept non-Celtic newcomers as religious equals, immediately placed these Catholic immigrants in an unfamiliar posture. To compound the issue, the local Catholic clergy was either incapable or unwilling to recognize the fundamental differences of language and tradition which distinguished Italians of different regions.

To the Italian immigrant whose social and religious lives had been molded by *campanilismo* and *la via vecchia,* this initial alienation from "their" church threatened their loyalty. This alienation also intensified a form of pure anticlericalism, which was always capable of distinguishing between "the clergy" and "the faith." While most Italians reluctantly accepted a subordinate role in the Catholic Church in Boston, many found it necessary to strike out against local religious practices. These Italian malcontents, though fundamentally loyal to the faith of their fathers, incurred the wrath and strained the administrative wisdom of Boston's Catholic hierarchy. Many others joined select Protestant[4] congregations, where they were made welcome.

The root cause of most of the friction between Italian and non-Italian Catholics was the *fabbriceria* system. The *fabbriceria* was a trustee system whereby prominent citizens gave major input into the administration of the parish. Even the financial affairs of the parish were within the sphere of these trustees. The *fabbriceria* system was commonly practiced throughout Italy in the late nineteenth century. In the United States, during the same time period, the Catholic bishops and pastors were totally responsible for the administration of the local parishes.[5] The *fabbriceria* system was actually similar to the manner in which many Protestant communities were administered in the United States. In spite of its democratic foundation, the very similarity to local Protestant custom, and its inherent challenge to the authority of the local Catholic hierarchy, made the *fabbriceria* system anathema in Boston.

While the *fabbriceria* system proved to be the greatest single source of conflict, Boston's North End Italians had other religious problems as well. Their relationship with the Catholic Church had been developed in an Italy where political unification enhanced existing anticlericalism,[6] and encouraged the growth of Freemasonry. Disastrous economic policies both before and after unification contributed to religious indifference. Disenchanted peasants, as well as disgruntled anarchists, socialists and republicans, viewed the church with suspicion. Many saw a wealthy institution whose priests managed to live in relative comfort while the plight of the peasants went unabated. In Italy, the clergy received salaries from a government which was exacting impossible taxes. Regular church attendance was generally viewed as a female activity,[7] while men attended church services only on holy days and special family occasions. Baptisms, weddings, and funerals held a particular significance. Religious education was generally poor, caused at least in part by the very low level of literacy among the southern peasant class. The old-world church was a social as well as religious institution. Since all social events and , through them, the perpetuation of *la via vecchia* were inextricably tied to the church's physical complex, anticlericalism did coexist alongside an intense loyalty to the village church.[8]

The Genoese, who were the earliest Italian Catholic immigrants to Boston, were quickly expected to accept local religious practices. Catholics in the United States were required to financially support both the clergy and the maintenance of church property. A "seat offering"[9] was required for church attendance. Monetary offerings for baptism and marriage ceremonies were expected. Parochial education for children was strongly encouraged. Regular church attendance by both men and women was the norm. Though these customs may not seem unreasonable to a modern American Catholic, it must be reiterated that the Genoese, and all Italian Catholic immigrants for that matter, were already convinced of the wealth of the Catholic Church. This "insistence" on monetary offerings and a pay-as-you-go school system from immigrants who often had to work seven days a week for survival certainly did very little to alter the anticlerical attitudes with which they arrived. The failure of the church hierarchy to allow lay input in the form of the *fabbriceria* system was viewed with equal hostility. The initial failure of these northern Italian Catholics to obtain Italian language services and social activities only added to the lack of understanding on both sides.

There were 12 Italian priests listed in the official diocesan record in 1866.[10] Though the post-Civil War period saw the development of special assignments in the diocese, all 12 were assigned to English-speaking ministries. In 1868, three members of the Order of Friars Minor (Franciscans),[11] Emiliano Gerbi, Vincent Borgialli, and Angelo Conterno received the distinction of being the first priests specifically, though not exclusively, assigned to an Italian language ministry in the Diocese of Boston.[12] Their ministry, however, did not include any specific work in the North End.

Saint Mary's Church, on Thatcher Street in the North End, founded by Bishop Benedict Fenwick in 1835, was the site of the first Italian congregation in Boston. In 1868 Simon Dompieri, a Jesuit priest, acted as assistant pastor of Saint Mary's Church. He was also spiritual head of the Italian congregation at the adjacent Saint Mary's Chapel[13] until it closed in 1873. Father Dompieri was the second Italian priest stationed at Saint Mary's since the Jesuits assumed the administration of that parish in 1847.[14] Though Father Francis DiMaria acted as pastor in 1863, both the parish records and archdiocesan archives fail to indicate any distinct Italian ministry prior to Father Dompieri's assignment.

The Italian congregation at Saint Mary's Chapel numbered fewer than 300. The chapel, located near the main church was of the small storefront variety so common among early immigrant groups.[15] Italians, accustomed to grandiose houses of worship in the old country, must have been disheartened by the drabness of Saint Mary's Chapel. Irrespective of the reasons given, the very inaccessibility of the more impressive Saint Mary's Church certainly stirred the sensibilities of these Italians.

The summer of 1873 was a turning point for Boston's Italian community. Their numbers had become sufficient to warrant a separate house of worship. Bishop John Williams[16] purchased the Free Will Baptist Meeting House on North Bennett Street for $25,000 on June 7, 1873.[17] After an investment of an additional $3,000 for what the Catholic archives describe as "fitting up for suitable service,"[18] the bishop offered the structure both to the Italian and Portuguese communities in the North End for a period of two years. Whichever of these two groups raised more money during that period was to gain exclusive use of the facility. Bishop Williams intended to appoint the Franciscan Friar Emiliano Gerbi[19] as Chaplain of the Boston Italians and pastor of the Italian community at Saint John the Baptist. The much respected Father Gerbi, however, died of tuberculosis[20] only three weeks after the church property was purchased.[21] Father Gerbi's colleague, Friar Angelo Conterno, was appointed to the Italian post at Saint John the Baptist's on July 16, 1873. Father John Ignazio Azevedo, a native of the Azores, was appointed pastor of the Portuguese congregation at that same church. Father Azevedo and his parishioners won the two year fundraising competition. They collected over $12,000, while their Italian counterparts managed to raise less than $10,000.[22] Thus, the Church of John the Baptist became a Portuguese National Parish in 1875. Even though the Italians were asked by Father Azevedo to remain, they were disappointed and still desired a place of worship which was truly their own. An undated entry in the Episcopal Register[23] records that: "at the end of the two year period the national group which raises the lesser amount of money would be allowed to take the funds they had collected, and use them towards the purchase of another place of worship". This option aided the Italians in making their decision to look elsewhere for a church.

In 1875, Friar Joachim Guerrini was chosen to replace Friar Conterno as Italian pastor of Saint John the Baptist. One of the reasons given[24] for the transfer was Father Guerrini's prior success as a fund raiser. It immediately became his task to find a new site for his restless congregation. They did not have long to wait. The Hooton Estate, at the corner of Prince and Hanover Streets, was purchased that same year for slightly less than $9,000.[25] This site, but one block from "the Portuguese church," measured only 74 feet by 30 feet. A small wood frame structure was erected on the land, and dedicated February 23, 1876, under the patronage of Saint Leonard of Port Maurice,[26] whose feast was celebrated on that date. The structure was modest but the ceremony was truly grand. A Solemn Mass was celebrated by Archbishop John Williams. The Franciscan superior, Friar Charles Vissani, came from

New York for the occasion. Father Paolino delivered the eulogy. Father Guerrini, the pastor, also participated in the ceremony.

Along with his responsiblities at the newly consecrated Saint Leonard's Church, Father Guerrini was also given the distinction of being the first priest specifically assigned to care for the Italian community of the entire archdiocese. The new church was the official church of all Italians—mostly Genoese with some Neapolitans—located throughout the archdiocese, and not just those living in the central city. Besides the 1,500 mostly Genoese community living in Boston proper in 1875,[27] in addition to North End Italians from Genoa, Parma, Piacenza, and Naples, Fr. Guerrini's flock included an additional 2,000 "Italians" scattered throughout the lower Merrimack Valley, the South Shore, and the area immediately surrounding the city of Boston— an area of more that 1,000 square miles. As if the task of administering to such a scattered group were not taxing enough, his work was made even more difficult by his religious superiors when he was specifically charged: *"Parochia est Italia, Confessiones auscultantur etiam in lingua Anglica"* ("The parish is Italian, [but] confessions should also be heard in English").[28] Father Guerrini was thus commissioned to care for the English-speaking community as well. It appears that the archbishop hoped to encourage the Italian congregation gradually to make a transition to the English language by this introduction of bilingualism at Saint Leonard's Church.

Father Guerrini, who had worked with an Irish congregation for the past fourteen years, soon found his weekly devotions to Saint Anthony attracting an ever-increasing non-Italian congregation. The Genoese community resented the care "their" priest was now required to give to the Irish community, and subsequently balked at his fundraising efforts to the point that he was unable to raise adequate capital to meet the running expenses of the parish. During a two-year tenure, Father Guerrini, who had previously been highly respected for his fiscal abilities, was so hard pressed to raise funds in the Genoese parish that his creditors obtained a warrant for his arrest.[29] This problem caused by Genoese regional pride as much as by the neglect of the pastor, increased the parish debt to more than $30,000. In October, 1878, Father Guerrini went to New York rather than face his creditors.[30] His superiors sent Father Boniface Bragantini[31] to settle the financial situation, and replace Father Guerrini as pastor of Saint Leonard's Church.

The administration of Father Bragantini (1878-1887) proved to be even more turbulent than that of his predecessor. The ever-increasing use of Saint Leonard's Church by the Irish community continued unabated. To compound the problems of the new pastor, the predominantly Genoese congregation witnessed an influx of "undesirable" southern Italians, causing centuries-old North-South hostilities to surface. As noted in chapter 1, the root cause of this hostility was cultural, linguistic, and racial, not necessarily in that order.

It soon became difficult to determine whether the Italian-Irish conflict, or the North Italian-South Italian hostility occupied more of Father Bragantini's attention.

The unwillingness of the North Italian population[32] to support Saint Leonard's Church to the satisfaction of the clergy both within the parish and at the archbishop's residence, coupled with the embarrassment of the Guerrini affair and the growing non-Italian presence in the church, made Father Bragantini's task almost impossible. The northern Italian merchant class, popularly identified as the Genoese,[33] wanted a greater say in the administration of the parish. They felt that the physical structure itself was too small, and certainly lacked the skilled decorative art to which they were accustomed. In 1884, they formed the *Societa' Cattolica Italiana*[34] to formalize plans for the purchase of Father Taylor's Seaman's Bethel in North Square,[35] or the erection of a new structure somewhere in the North End. Early in 1884, a delegation from the *Societa' Cattolica Italiana,* henceforth known as *Societa' San Marco,* discussed plans for a new church with Father Bragantini, the new pastor of Saint Leonard's. He agreed that there was need for a larger church, suggesting the purchase of the Bethel in North Square because it would be more economical than building a new structure. Also, it certainly would be large enough for the congregation. The committee agreed, but insisted that the new church had to be structured according to the *fabbriceria* system to which they were accustomed. The pastor balked at this suggestion because it was contrary to local practice, and it would have handed virtual control of the church to the Genoese community, creating even greater friction within the now diverse[36] Italian community in the North End. The ensuing events became so controversial that it took the assistance of a bishop in Italy,[37] the action of the Franciscan superior in New York, and the intervention of the Vatican[38] in Rome to resolve.

While a more detailed study of the remaining five years of this controversy would be of value, for my purpose it is sufficient to add that the rift between Father Bragantini and the Genoese community soon became irreconcilable. Archbishop Williams entered the picture, when, in June, 1885, the *Societa' San Marco* purchased the Bethel[39] without the permission of the diocese—a violation of church law.

The conflict with the *Societa' San Marco* was not unique[40] to the North End of Boston, nor to the Italian Catholic community there. What was unique was the ultimate resolution of the crisis. In February, 1889, Bishop Francesco Satolli was sent by Pope Leo XIII on a tour of Italian missions in North America, at least partially in response to the failures of the 1884 Third Plenary Council of Baltimore to address the issue of how Italian Catholics could be better cared for (see note 40). When Bishop Satolli visited the dilapidated Beverley Street Chapel, which the *Societa' San Marco* had been "allowed" to use for several years, he was appalled, and subsequently described it to Pope Leo as a "cave."[41] As a result, a new round of negotiations opened up in February, 1890. Three months later Archbishop Williams agreed that Saint Mark's Church could be opened for worship.

Joseph Tassinari,[42] the present president of the *Societa' San Marco,* reflecting the earlier statements of his father and uncle, described the compromise to me in a September, 1979, interview:

> The archbishop was stubborn, but we won in the long run. What eventually happened was that the property in North Square—both church and rectory—remained in the name of the Saint Mark Society. The archbishop has the legal right to take the property from us at his discretion, provided—and this is a *Big IF*—we agree with either the price or accept the alternate site he wants to provide us with. To my knowledge, we are the only lay organization in the United States legally to own a Catholic Church even today. We also won on the Franciscan issue. The archbishop allowed us to keep the Scalabrini Fathers. The church is still run by the *fabbriceria* system because all financial matters must meet with my approval and that of the executive board. We are also unique in this situation. One thing Archbishop Williams did win out on was that we could not use the church if we did not change the name. I guess the name "Saint Mark's Church" must have given him some sleepless nights. The society agreed upon the name "Sacred Heart *Italian* Church" in 1890.

The history of the beginnings of the two Italian churches in the North End continually reflected the inner tensions at work in the burgeoning Italian community. One of my concerns in this work, however, has been to determine whether these tensions between Italian subcultures were reflected throughout the entire period under study. The controversies between the Genoese and southern Italian community which characterized North End life in the early years was clearly measurable, but what of the religious friction which marked the "post San Marco period"? A study of the marriage patterns among North End Italians suggests that a form of *campanilismo* had been at work in the two North End Italian Churches until 1930. Specifically, individuals from different South Italian provinces consistently married in only one of the two churches in question, even though the structures were but one short block apart. If this continuation of old-world provincial loyalties extended to marriage patterns, why could it not be measured by some other means as well? I consequently decided to study the baptismal records in both Saint Leonard's Church and Sacred Heart Church to determine whether *campanilismo* —a form of "religious enclavism"—was at work throughout the entire period, and not just until 1890, as the San Marco incident had clearly demonstated.

While the number of marriage ceremonies in the two churches from 1873 to 1929[43] had been impressive, the number of baptisms is staggering. During those years, there were 70,996 total baptisms: 42,872 at Sacred Heart Church, and 28,124 at Saint Leonard's Church. From 1900 to 1929, each church averaged 15 baptisms per week. For the purpose of continuity, I decided again

Plate 5. St. John the Baptist Church, North Bennett Street, Boston, 1880

Plate 6. Fr. John Azevedo, Portuguese Pastor, St. John the Baptist Church, 1873

Plate 7. Rev. Francis Zaboglio, First Pastor of Sacred Heart Church, Boston, 1890

Plate 8. Rev. Domenic Vincentini, Sacred Heart Church, Boston, 1910

Plate 9. Most Reverend John Williams, D.D.,
          Archbishop of Boston, 1866-1907

Plate 10. Saint Stephen's Church, Boston, 1880

Plate 11. Sacred Heart Church, Boston (Formerly
          Fr. Taylor's Seamen's Bethel), 1890

Plate 12. Second Church of Saint Leonard of Port Maurice, Boston, 1887

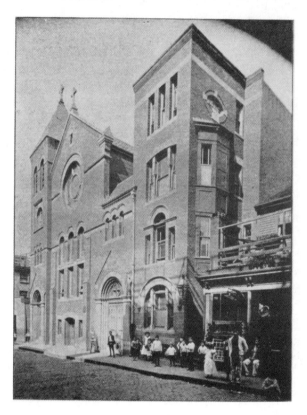

Plate 13.   Founders of Società San Marco with Father Francis
Zaboglio, 1889

Plate 14.   Dedication of New Facade of Sacred Heart Church,
            North Square, Boston, November 26, 1911

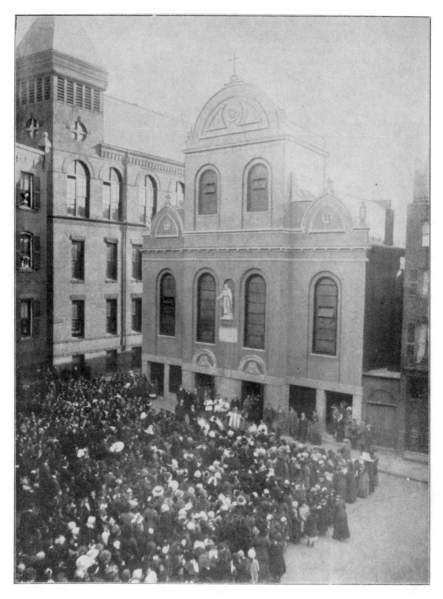

Plate 15.   Society of St. John Berchmans, Sacred Heart Church,
North Square, Boston, 1903

Plate 16. School for Young Homemakers, Sacred Heart Church,
North Square, Boston, 1916

Plate 17. Gymnasium for Young Boys, Saint Leonard of Port
Maurice Church, Prince Street, Boston, 1916

to use 1899, 1909, 1919, and 1929 as sample years for analysis. The number of baptisms during the four years under study was 7,967, representing 11.2 percent of the total number of baptisms in both churches from 1873 to 1929.

While this study clearly identified the "place of birth" of both parents of the child being baptized, it did suffer from several limitations. First and foremost, it is difficult to utilize baptismal records to identify the existence and location of "enclaves," for no addresses were given. Fortunately, the existence and location of "enclaves" had been measured in other ways. The second handicap was that both churches failed to follow any regular pattern of identification of "place of birth" of the parents of the baby. In some instances, towns were given, with no mention of province or region. In other instances, only the province or region was recorded. As had been the case with my study of marriage records, a careful identification of the location of Italian towns had to be carried out before any interpretation could be made. This irregularity of the recorded information was certainly more pronounced in the records of Saint Leonard's Church. Fortunately, unlike the shortcomings of its marriage records, baptismal records did contain some "place of birth" information of the parents as early as 1899.

While this study of baptismal records could not provide information concerning enclaves, it certainly provided information concerning *campanilismo*.[44] The identification of the towns of southern Italy most represented in each church's sacramental files clearly showed distinctions worth analyzing.

In 1899, there were 976 baptisms at Sacred Heart Church, of which 947 (or 97 percent) were children of first generation Italians. The total number of baptisms of children of southern Italians was 722 (or 74 percent). Two hundred and fifty four baptisms were of northern Italian children (or 26 percent). The southern Italian Province most often mentioned by 1899 was Avellino, (see map 3), accounting for 371 baptisms, or 38 percent of the total. The neighboring provinces of Benevento (8 percent) and Caserta (6 percent) also placed prominently. Sicilian provinces acounted for only 14 percent of the total number of Sacred Heart baptisms—136 out of 976. The north Italian provinces most often represented were Genoa and Piacenza, with Milan a close third.

The 1899 records for Saint Leonard's Church revealed that 451 children were baptized that year with 93.7 percent (422) of that total being first generation Italian-American. The total number of baptisms of southern Italian children was 443, or 98.3 percent of the total. There were four non-Italian baptisms (.88 percent), and an equal number of northern Italians—all from Genoa. Of the 443 southern Italian baptisms, 137 (30.9 percent) were from the province of Avellino, which again was the most often represented southern Italian province. Sicily accounted for 77 baptisms (17 percent). A pattern was quickly apparent when towns within the Province of Avellino were listed in each church. It must be restated, however, that while "town" or "village" designation was not given, when it was mentioned, different communities were mentioned in each church. For example, Candida, Avellino, was recorded nine times—all of which were at Saint Leonard's Church. Mirabella Eclano,Avellino, had 16 baptisms—14 of which were at Saint Leonard's Church. The towns of Taurasi and Chiusano San Domenico, both in Avellino, were only in the Sacred Heart files 90 percent of the time.

The year 1909 revealed similar tendencies. Sacred Heart Church had 1,517 baptisms. Of that total, 1,243 (81.9 percent) were southern Italian, 262 (17.2 percent) were northern Italian, and 12 (.79 percent) were non-Italian. The southern Italian provinces most often mentioned were Avellino, Campania (27.2 percent), Messina, Sicily (11.8 percent) Palermo, Sicily (4.1 percent), and Cosenza, Calabria (3.3 percent). Taurasi and Chiusano San Domenico again dominated the files. The Sicilian town of Sciacca in Girgenti appeared in the 1909 Sacred Heart file, but failed to be mentioned in that of Saint Leonard for the same year. In 1909, Saint Leonard's Church recorded 723 baptisms, 94.5 percent of whom were children of southern Italians, while 5 percent involved North Italians, and .5 percent non-Italians. The most frequently mentioned southern Italian provinces were Avellino, Campania (39.4 percent), Messina, Sicily (7.7 percent), and Pescara, Abruzzi (5.8 percent). In this case, I observed a continuation of the dominance of Mirabella Eclano, Avellino, in the Saint Leonard records, and a much higher percentage of Abruzzesi than in the Sacred Heart files.

The year 1919 contained few surprises. Sacred Heart Church revealed a baptism record of 1,440, with 191 (13.3 percent) northern Italian and 1,249 (86.7 percent) southern Italian. There were no non-Italian baptisms in 1919. Avellino accounted for 22.2 percent of all Sacred Heart baptisms. Other southern provinces represented were Benevento, Campania (4.2 percent), Messina, Sicily (10.2 percent), Caltanisetta, Sicily (8.5 percent), and Siracusa, Sicily (3.7 percent). Parma and Milan in northern Italy were the most represented in that category.

In the Saint Leonard files for the same year, distinct differences were soon apparent. For example, Siracusa, Sicily, did not have a single entry. The Abruzzese province of Campobasso (6.5 percent) was the Abruzzese province most frequently mentioned, while it received no mention in the Sacred Heart files. Trapani, Sicily, was mentioned 3.5 percent of the time in the Saint Leonard's files, and only 0.9 percent in Sacred Heart's. Of all 1919 baptisms at Saint Leonard's Church, 94.1 percent were southern Italian, and 5.9 percent were northern Italian. Again, there were no non-Italian baptisms. Saint Leonard's Church had a total of 1,205 baptisms that year.

In 1929, there was a noticeable diminution of total baptisms in both churches, with only 1,655 recorded. Sacred Heart Church accounted for 878 of that total. Of these, 92.5 percent were southern Italian, and 7.5 percent were northern Italian. The most often represented southern Italian provinces were Avellino, Campania (10.6 percent), Caltanisetta, Sicily (7.5 percent), and Messina, Sicily (3.7 percent).

The Saint Leonard files for the same year showed that all of its 777 baptisms were southern Italian. The province of Avellino accounted for a percentage twice as high (22.3 percent) as that in the Sacred Heart files. The town of Mirabella Eclano in Avellino accounted for the greatest percentage of Avellinesi at Saint Leonard's while it was rarely mentioned at Sacred Heart. Other measurable differences were that while Caltanisetta and Messina, Sicily, were the most often represented Sicilian provinces at Sacred Heart, Trapani (6.2 percent) and Palermo (6.2 percent) were the most often mentioned at Saint Leonard's Church, where both Messina and Caltanisetta were barely measurable.

The baptism records of both Sacred Heart and Saint Leonard Churches for the four years studied are in complete agreement with all other material developed for this work. While these records did not identify the addresses of North End Italians, they did illustrate that Italians of specific provinces and villages most often frequented one of the two churches under study. With the exception of northern Italians who frequented Sacred Heart Church much more frequently than Saint Leonard's—this is understandable in light of the history of these institutions—both churches numbered southern Italians among their faithful in similar percentages. What did emerge, however, was that the "smaller" the unit under study became, the more obvious were the distinctions observed. This is in keeping with my earliest findings[44] concerning the existence of *campanilismo* in southern Italian villages.

Oral testimony concerning loyalty of North End Italian residents to either Sacred Heart or Saint Leonard's Church offered further validation. When asked whether they attended church regularly at only one Italian house of worship, some of the answers given were: "Of course. Our family belonged to Saint Leonard's since the early days,"[45] and, "I don't think I have been in Saint Leonard's for ten years. Sacred Heart is my church."[46] I was intrigued by the loyalty these North End Italian residents revealed to a church which was barely one block away from another Italian Catholic religious structure. I pursued this line of questioning with all of those interviewed. Alfredo Tassinari,[47] while 103 years old at the time of our August, 1977 interview, lucidly described this loyalty in the following manner:

> One thing you have to understand, young man, is that we did not get along too well. Italians generally mistrusted each other because they did not have to get along in the old country for survival. Their families were everything. In the North End, Italians generally went to either Sacred Heart or Saint Leonard's. This was true of whole families. I remember that I would have gotten very upset if a member of my family went to church at Saint

Leonard's. It just was not our church. The only time this would be allowed would be if we had to attend a funeral or wedding of a friend, and, of course, on Holy Thursday, when everyone visits as many churches as possible. (A custom practiced throughout the Catholic Church prior to the Second Vatican Council.)

This "loyalty" described by Alfredo Tassinari was expected as recently as my North End childhood in the late forties and early fifties. Even though the two churches celebrated Mass thirty minutes apart from each other, no self-respecting member of either congregation would attend the "wrong" church, for fear of suffering the wrath of some family member. It must be pointed out that this was true in spite of the fact that both ceremonies were identical in substance and form. More tolerance was shown if, infrequently, for the sake of convenience, a person attended one of the neighborhood's "American churches"—Saint Stephen's or Saint Mary's—but certainly not the "wrong" Italian church.

Both the earliest history of the North End Italian churches, and their baptismal records, reveal a tension among Italian ranks, and a strong loyalty to "their church," much as had been the case in the old world villages. Sacred Heart and Saint Leonard's Churches took on distinct characteristics as a result, in spite of their geographical proximity.

The history of religious groups—often akin to social clubs—in the neighborhood also reveals a strong retention of old-world practices. Many of these groups were identified with either Italian church, where their religious and social activities took place. A study of church records, contemporary literature,[48] and testimony of North End Italian clergy revealed that there were no less than 50 religious societies[49] in the North End Italian community during the years of my study. In order to make an analysis more manageable, I chose 1910 as the sample year of analysis. Most of the subcultures settling in the North End had already stabilized. Therefore, it is possible to identify subcultural groups and their religious societies without slighting any major subculture.

Some general observations should first be made. Most of the Italian religious societies initially provided a physical place where members could congregate. They were located initially in the church or school hall of either Sacred Heart or Saint Leonard's Church, and, later, may have moved to a building owned by the group. In most cases, the organization was formed to cater to the spiritual and temporal needs of individuals from a specific province or region of Italy. The patron saint of the organization was usually the same as that of the town from which most of its members came. A "chapel" to the patron saint of the group was erected either in the society's "club," or at the church where their religious activities took place.

In 1961, nonagenarian Rev. Pio Parolin, who was ordained a priest by Bishop Scalabrini in 1901, and who served as parish priest at Sacred Heart Church at the turn of the century, reminisced about these societies:

> They did a lot of good in the early days. Each group catered to individuals from a specific area. They helped out with spiritual, moral, and financial support for their members.

Rev. Joseph Invernizzi, the pastor of Sacred Heart Church during the 1960s also described the North End religious societies in a November 7, 1977 interview:

> They were well-intentioned and necessary groups in the days when large numbers of Italians settled in the North End. They provided a place where these poor, displaced persons could come and feel at home among people from their own Italian provinces. The money they raised from dues and from their yearly religious festivals often helped the more destitute among them. They were genuinely religious organizations as well. Somewhere along the way, these groups unfortunately lost their direction, and those that now exist perform very little charitable work either among their own *paesani,* or with the community as a whole.

Again, there is a mention of the importance of *paesani* in the everyday life of these immigrants.

The earliest Italian societies in the North End, as expected, were made up of individuals from northern Italy, particularly Genoa. Prior to 1880, two societies were formed. Both of these, *Mutuo Soccorso* and *Italiana Colombo* were created by Genoese for the temporal care of their own immigrants. The *Societa' San Marco,* which we have already discussed, was established in 1884. Three other societies, *Maria Santissima Ausiliatrice* (1889), *Bersaglieri* (1891), and *Ligure* (1894) were also formed by and for Genoese. The first six religious groups in the North End, therefore, were northern Italian, in keeping with my research conclusions. These names tell much about the make-up of the organizations in question. *Mutuo Soccorso* literally means "mutual aid," and *Maria Santissima Ausiliatrice* means "Most Holy Mary and Helper." While these two groups are no longer in existence, Joseph Tassinari, the current president of the *Societa' San Marco* said that their activities, though not as successful as those of Saint Mark, were similar in nature. They provided assistance for recently arrived immigrants such as helping to locate housing and finding employment. Ligure is the region of Italy where Genoa is located, and *Italiana Colombo* was named after Genoa's favorite son, Christopher Columbus.

The first mention of southern Italians in the religious organizations of the North End was with the formation of *Maria Santissima Ausiliatrice,* created in 1894 by Avellinesi who worshipped at Saint Leonard's Church. All of the organizations mentioned thus far had been affiliated with Sacred Heart Church in North Square. With the exception of this group at Saint Leonard's Church, no other religious society catered to the southern Italian population of the North End prior to 1900.

An organization under the patronage of *Saint Ciriaco,* the patron saint of the Marches area of Italy (former Papal States) was formed in 1896. The formation of the *Conte di Torino* society by Piedmontesi of northern Italy in 1897 reinforced the existence of northern Italians in the neighborhood prior to 1900.

It is of particular significance to note that just as there was only one southern Italian society in the North End prior to 1900, only three of the thirty new societies formed in the ensuing decade were for northern Italians: the 1903 *Amerigo Vespucci* society of Florentines, the 1906 *San Pietro di Roma* society of Romans, and the 1907 *Vittorio Emanuele* society of Piedmontesi. The *San Pietro di Roma* groups met regularly at Sacred Heart Church,[50] while the other two groups did not seem to have any religious affiliation.[51]

Of the remaining twenty-seven new groups organized from 1900 to 1910, twelve were made up primarily of Avellinesi, five were Sicilian, four were Neapolitan, two were Calabrese, and only one was Abruzzese. According to the 1910 membership statistics, as developed by Anna Martellone,[52] 36.23 percent, or 1,270 out of 3,505, of all society members were Avellinesi. This is remarkably similar to the 31.10 percent combined intramarriage figure of Avellinesi in both North End Italian churches the previous year, as well as the 33.14 percent combined figure for baptisms of Avellinesi at both North End churches.

The names of the southern Italian societies were very revealing. As had been the case with their northern Italian counterparts, the southern Italians chose names which identified closely to the old world community with which they were familiar. Consequently, names such as Taurasi (1907), Montevergine (1906), Etna (1906), Imera (1905), Chiusano San Domenico (1904), Benevento (1903), and Montefalcione (1900) all of which were southern Italian towns, were adopted as society names. Other names were those of the patron saint of the village, such as *Maria Santissima Buon Consiglio* (Candida, Avellino), *San Giovanni di Messina* (Messina, Sicily), and *Stella della Calabria* (Cosenza, Calabria).

While much work still needs to be done concerning the existence of Italian religious and social clubs in Boston's North End, my study has revealed that their existence closely followed the religious and social patterns established by *campanilismo* in the old world villages, and most recently manifest in the social structure of the North End's two Italian Catholic Churches. The existence and organizational structure of these groups greatly coincided with the religious records already analyzed. Fortunately, six of these organizations presently exist: *Mutuo Socccorso* (Sacred Heart), *San Marco* (Sacred Heart), *Maria Santissima Buon Consiglio, San Antonio* (Saint Leonard's), *San Rocco* (Sacred Heart), and *Montevergine* (Sacred Heart). The existence of these groups in 1981 has made it possible to interview past members, and to ask about records. Unfortunately, however, with the exception of *San Marco,* which always kept adequate records, the other organizations failed to maintain records of their past history. Even interviews are well nigh impossible, because present members are primarily elderly ladies who recall the weekly or monthly devotions, and little else. Because of this, it seems that until documentation other than the Saint Mark Society records, and Leveroni's 1913 history of Sacred Heart Church are located, a more complete history of the religious societies of the North End cannot be completed.

This study of the North End Italian Catholic Community has helped identify that each church was organized in response to friction within the Italian community over both the method and location of its religious services; that each church continued to attract Italians from specific villages within similar Italian provinces; that each church commanded a loyalty which made it unthinkable for one of its members to frequent the alternate Italian Catholic church; and finally, that all of these patterns seemed to be similar to the forms of *campanilismo* which dominated the lives of the *contadini* in the villages of the *Mezzogiorno.* While the location of their enclaves did not determine which of the two churches a particular group would frequent, individuals from specific Italian villages worshipped *en masse* in only Sacred Heart or Saint Leonard's Church, reflecting a conscious decision to associate exclusively with *paesani* even when addressing the Deity.

5

Paesani Work Here

Historians have not yet adequately analyzed North End Italian employment patterns. There are several reasons for this. First, here as elsewhere, stereotypes[1] have been accepted too readily. Second, the impact of "enclaves" and "chain occupation processes" have not been applied to analyses of this experience. Third, oral history, which has only relatively recently been utilized and accepted, has not been tapped as a source.

This chapter will show that North End Italians held a variety of jobs, both menial and professional, and that within the framework of that employment, they managed to maintain many of the old-world values brought to Boston from their Italian villages. While labor agents did not play a very significant role in the maintenance of a chain-employment process among the community's Italian population, Italians did manage to work with their *paesani* by choice. This practice, constantly nourished by their compulsion to preserve *la via vecchia* and to protect *la famiglia,* did, in effect, create a chain employment pattern wherever possible.

This chapter is not an analysis of any particular enclave, nor is it an in-depth study of a particular place of employment. While research in these areas is certainly desirable, the lack of sufficient available data[2] has made such research impractical at this time. Only nine of the ninety-eight companies identified in the 1909 *Boston Directory* (see Appendix) as employers of North End Italians are still in existence in 1980. Only one of these—Joseph Langone, Undertakers—was of any assistance in identifying its employees from the beginning of the century. In this case, while most of those identified were Avellinesi, the sample was too small to be significant. Cafe Marliave and the Parker House Hotel also employed too few Italians to have made any records significant, had they existed. The Aberthaw Construction Company did not have any employee records available from the beginning of the century, nor did W. Baker and Company, Wm. Schrafft Company, or New England Confectionary Company.

The *Boston City Directories* and oral testimony from surviving members of the North End Italian community help in presenting a glimpse into the private world of these immigrants. In order to provide continuity with the dates investigated in the previous chapter, the years 1899, 1909, 1919, and 1929 will again be analyzed for the identification of trends in employment statistics.

One of the problems encountered here is that the *Boston City Directory,* like the Sacramental Records used earlier, did not always contain complete or accurate data. For example, rather than listing the place of employment, many entries showed an industrial type of job. In other instances, four or five men in a given family were listed with no visible means of support. Except for those who had just arrived in Boston, this would appear to be most unusual for a period in our history when there was no public means of support for those who were unemployed. Even though the family network would have provided for a member's well being even if he were employed, it must be restated that, to an Italian, the male must support the family by the sweat of his brow. This was the measure of his worth.[3] It was thus safe to assume in these instances that the census taker was given incomplete information because the Italians did not want to divulge what they considered their own business, or because they were hiding something, or that they did not fully understand the interrogator's questions. In my estimation, another problem with the *City Directory* is that names were often incorrectly recorded. My paternal grandfather, for instance, was incorrectly listed Di Marco rather than De Marco from 1917 to 1926. Mistakes seemed to have been carried over for many years. One other example brought this to the extreme. My maternal grandmother, who was illiterate like so many of the immigrants, never had her name listed correctly in the *Directory.* She lived in Boston for sixty-two years. A great-uncle was listed in the *Directory* for four years after he permanently returned to Italy. The obvious question arises: if the *Boston City Directory* is unreliable,[4] why use it? Like the *Dillingham Commission Report*[5] and the Sacramental Records, the *Boston City Directory* is a piece of the mosaic which must be observed if the entire picture is to be understood. It will help to verify other data, and might raise questions which the other data studied thus far failed to ask.

The *Boston City Directory* lists its entries in alphabetical order by surname, with street addresses and type and place of employment. Neither nationality nor neighborhood are listed. The absence of these designations makes a knowledge of both North End street names and Italian surnames essential.[3] My research method involved the selective taking of Italian surnames, using every letter of the alphabet, from among the two thousand pages of each directory studied. While this method assured that close to 10 percent of the declared work force would, in fact, be analyzed, it did not allow for a true random sample, which would have required the use of a computer first to withdraw all North End Italian names from the *Directory,* and only then randomly to pick every tenth name, for example. My method, on the other hand, did allow for some objectivity because, by selecting names from throughout the alphabet, I was assured of analyzing individuals from throughout southern Italy, where relatively few surnames are common in any one village or town. Based on my "selective" sample, some conclusions can be drawn: (a) more than one hundred types of jobs held by North End Italians were found in the *Boston City Directory*; (b) while most of these jobs were menial, many professional positions were listed as well; (c) almost universally, more than half of the individuals listed with a particular surname were involved in the same type of occupation.

Of the 102 occupations identified by me in the *Boston City Directory* for North End Italians, twelve were chosen for analysis: (1) construction work, (2) barber, (3) fruit vendor/grocer, (4) baker, (5) fisherman, (6) assorted hotel employment, (7) restaurant work, (8) *padrone,* (9) doctor, (10) lawyer, (11) confectioner, (12) tailor/seamstress.

In no other category of employment, with the possible exception of "barber," was there such a complete domination of one form of employment by all members of a family as there was in the "construction" category. Because of the nature of the work, the advantages of similar language and values were all-important. The same dialect could be used by all workers in the beginning, and the family welfare was enhanced as more members of the family joined the business in subsequent years. This provided for a form of familial well-being, which was so very common in Italy. It was a way of perpetuating *la via vecchia* by providing for the protection of the most sacred of all units, *la famiglia.*

The *Boston City Directory* listed 808 of the 3,235 individuals (27.2 percent) taken in my sample as employed in construction. The supervisory position of foreman accounted for an additional 1.5 percent for the four sample years.

Two of the individuals most representative of this trade during the years studied were octogenarians James Sablone,[6] and Joseph Cassia.[7] They gave similar answers to the question: "What kind of individuals did you hire when you began a construction project?" The late James Sablone (see Plates 25-29), who began to work in the construction trade in 1909 was a retired sewerage foreman from Pescara, Abruzzi, at the time of our May, 1975 interview. He said:

> They had to be hard working. We usually had greatest success with married men or guys who had families in Italy. . . . Sicilians didn't work too hard. We had men—even whole families—from the same *paese* in Abruzzi, or Avellino, sometimes. We very often worked with men supplied by Rossi Brothers Construction of Roslindale. They were all Abruzzesi like us.

Table 2. Occupational Sampling of North End Italians*

	1899 No.	%	1909 No.	%	1919 No.	%	1929 No.	%	Totals No.	%
Accountant	0		0		2	.243	5	.538	7	.216
Actor	1	.186	2	.211	0		1	.108	4	.124
Artist	0		0		1	.122	2	.215	3	.093
Baker	4	.746	14	1.47	14	1.70	16	1.72	48	1.48
Barber	56	10.4	124	13.1	52	6.32	61	6.56	293	9.06
Bartender	5	.933	7	.739	2	.243	0		14	.433
Blacksmith	3	.559	4	.422	4	.486	2	.215	13	.402
Bookbinder	0		3	.317	2	.243	2	.215	7	.216
Bootblack	12	2.24	9	.951	8	.972	6	.645	35	1.08
Bottler	0		12	1.26	1	.122	2	.215	15	.464
Brassworker	0		0		2	.243	1	.108	3	.093
Breweryworker	0		3	.317	1	.122	0		4	.124
Bricklayer	2	.373	6	.634	6	.729	8	.860	22	.680
Butcher	0		3	.317	8	.972	9	.968	20	.618
Cabinetmaker	2	.373	7	.739	5	.607	8	.860	22	.680
Canner	0		17	1.79	0		0		17	.526
Carpenter	10	1.87	8	.845	7	.851	9	.968	34	1.05
Chairmaker	0		5	.528	6	.729	8	.860	19	.587
Chef	0		3	.317	5	.607	8	.860	16	.495
Cigarmaker	3	.559	4	.422	2	.243	5	.538	14	.433
Clerk	24	4.48	19	2.00	36	4.37	39	4.19	118	3.65
Confectioner	15	2.80	23	2.43	29	3.52	37	3.98	104	3.21
Cooper	0		0		1	.122	0		1	.031
Dentist	0		0		1	.122	1	.108	2	.062
Driver	2	.373	17	1.79	9	1.09	14	1.51	42	1.30
Electrician	0		0		2	.243	5	.538	7	.216
Elevatorman	0		0		4	.486	6	.645	10	.309
Engineer	0		0		3	.364	5	.538	8	.247
Fireman	0		0		4	.486	6	.645	10	.309
Fisherman	1	.186	14	1.47	16	1.94	23	2.47	54	1.67
Floorlayer	0		5	.528	5	.608	0		10	.309
Florist	0		0		5	.608	6	.645	11	.340
Foreman	0		3	.317	15	1.82	24	2.58	42	1.30
Fruit Vendor	34	6.34	38	4.01	16	1.94	28	3.01	116	3.59
Gardener	0		3	.317	0		2	.215	5	.155
Glass Polisher	1	.186	0		0		0		1	.031
Grocer	20	3.73	12	1.26	23	2.79	27	2.90	82	2.53
Hatmaker	0		0		3	.364	4	.430	7	.216
Hod Carrier	0		2	.211	1	.122	3	.323	6	.185
Hotel Clerk	1	.186	9	.951	8	.972	6	.645	24	.742
Hotel Manager	0		0		1	.122	5	.538	6	.185
Hurdy Gurdy	0		2	.211	1	.122	2	.215	5	.155
Instrument Maker	5	.933	3	.317	6	.729	8	.860	22	.680
Interpreter	0		7	.739	1	.122	3	.323	11	.340
Janitor	0		0		7	.851	12	1.30	19	.587
Jeweler	2	.373	0		0		3	.323	5	.155
Judge	0		1	.105	0		0		1	.031
Junk Dealer	1	.186	0		0		0		1	.031
Labor Agent	0		3	.317	0		0		3	.093

Table 2. Occupational Sampling of North End Italians *(Continued)*

	1899 No.	%	1909 No.	%	1919 No.	%	1929 No.	%	Totals No.	%
Laborer	196	36.6	223	23.5	250	30.4	211	22.7	880	27.2
Laundryman	0		0		1	.122	3	.323	4	.124
Lawyer	0		5	.528	3	.365	6	.645	14	.433
Leather Tanner	0		7	.739	1	.122	2	.215	10	.309
Liquor Merchant	3	.560	0		10	1.22	0		13	.402
Longshoreman	0		7	.739	4	.486	11	1.18	22	.680
Macaronimaker	0		7	.739	1	.122	3	.323	11	.340
Machinist	0		4	.422	11	1.34	2	2.26	36	1.11
Marble Cutter	12	2.24	28	2.95	6	.729	4	.430	50	1.55
Mariner	2	.373	0		0		2	.215	4	.124
Mason	12	2.24	0		13	1.58	19	2.04	44	1.36
Mattressmaker	1	.186	3	.317	2	.243	2	.215	8	.247
Milkman	0		0		1	.122	3	.323	4	.124
Molder	0		3	.317	1	.122	1	.108	5	.155
Mosaic Worker	2	.373	9	.951	2	.243	4	.430	17	.526
Musician	0		7	.739	7	.851	11	1.18	25	.772
Painter	4	.746	7	.739	5	.608	9	.968	25	.772
Peddler	9		7	.739	7	.851	6	.645	29	.896
Pharmacist	1	.186	0		5	.608	7	.753	13	.402
Photographer	1	.186	0		1	.122	3	.323	5	.155
Physician	3	.559	6	.634	4	.486	3	.323	16	.495
Plasterer	2	.373	11	1.16	5	.608	3	.323	21	.649
Platemaker	1	.186	0		0		0		1	.031
Plumber	0		0		8	.972	10	1.08	18	.556
Poolroom Attendent	1	.186	4	.422	1	.122	2	.215	8	.247
Porter	2	.373	4	.422	10	1.22	12	1.30	28	.866
Pressman	3	.560	5	.528	4	.486	4	.430	16	.495
Priest	2	.373	3	.317	1	.122	3	.323	9	.278
Printer	3	.560	5	.528	3	.365	4	.430	15	.464
Realtor	0		3	.317	1	.122	2	.215	6	.185
Restaurant-worker	4	.746	18	1.90	7	.851	21	2.26	50	1.55
Roofer	0		7	.739	6	.729	0		13	.402
Rubberworker	0		0		6	.729	0		6	.185
Salesman	0		8	.845	7	.851	6	.645	2	.649
Shoemaker	18	3.36	68	7.18	43	5.22	38	4.09	167	5.16
Soapmaker	0		0		1	.122	0		1	.031
Soapstoneworker	0		4	.422	1	.122	0		5	.155
Stenographer	0		0		1	.122	2	.215	3	.093
Stone Polisher	8	1.49	8	.845	3	.364	4	.430	23	.711
Student	0		0		2	.243	3	.323	5	.155
Tailor	19	3.54	42	4.43	22	2.67	29	3.12	112	3.46
Teacher	3	.560	8	.845	4	.486	6	.645	21	.649
Teamster	5	.933	0		6	.729	4	.430	15	.464
Tileworker	0		0		1	.122	0		1	.031
Tinsmith	5	.933	12	1.26	0		0		17	.526
Train Porter	0		8	.845	0		2	.215	10	.309
Undertaker	0		3	.317	0		2	.215	5	.155

Table 2. Occupational Sampling of North End Italians *(Continued)*

	1899 No.	%	1909 No.	%	1919 No.	%	1929 No.	%	Totals No.	%
Waiter	2	.373	0		5	.608	7	.753	14	.433
Welder	0		0		1	.122	0		1	.031
Wiper	2	.373	1	.105	0		0		3	.093
Wireworker	0		11	1.16	0		2	.215	13	.402
Woodworker	6	1.12	8	.845	0		2	.215	13	.402
Writer	0		0		1	.122	2	.215	3	.093
TOTALS—	536	100	946	100	823	100	930	100	3235	100

* See *Boston City Directory,* 1899, 1909, 1919, 1929. The *Directory* is organized in a strict alphabetical order of surnames citywide.

Joseph Cassia (see Plate 33) worked as a general laborer as early as 1912, when he first migrated from Siracusa, Sicily. He later became a carpentry foreman. He said:

> We worked mostly with *paesani* from Siracusa, Sicily. They lived down on North Street in those days. You always knew what to expect. . . . You could understand what they were saying and thinking. We all had to work hard. We sometimes worked with the Irish, but we didn't get along too well. They did not work as hard as we did. I do remember one Irish boss many years ago who treated us well. I think his name was John. That's right, John Sullivan. We worked well with the Jews and the Poles, when we had to.

Joseph Tassinari,[8] a septuagenarian from Genoa, had uncles in the construction trades. He said:

> They always went everywhere for jobs. One week or one month they would be in Maine, then Connecticut or down 'the Cape' (Cape Cod). They went wherever the work was. It was a hard life but they had to do it for their families. This was common among the North End workers fifty or sixty years ago.

Most of the construction companies that the Italians worked for were subcontracting companies made up primarily or exclusively of family members and *paesani*. Louis Reppucci,[9] whose parents migrated from Avellino in 1906, was one of the brothers of Reppucci Construction, founded in 1912 and heavily relying on incoming migration from Avellino. He remembered his family business as just one of many such firms set up to provide a means of employment for the entire extended family. Some members actually did the construction, while others worked on the books or acted as a secretary. He also said that they often travelled great distances for extended periods of time.

Barbering was another area of employment where strong provincial ties remained intact throughout the entire period, the *Directory* identifying 9.06 percent of those studied in our sample. Most barber entries contained many of the same names and individuals living at the same address. "Grande & Sons," "Vero & Sons," and "DiBenedetto & Sons" were very common. Prior to 1905, barbers' licenses were not required in Massachusetts. Even after that date, a candidate merely had to apprentice under a licensed barber. Steady business, regular hours, limited restrictions, and a respectable income made this an ideal male family business. Its importance among the North End Italians was evident in a 1905 page one headline in the local Italian newspaper: "License Law for Barbers—to protect hygiene—Not Directed at Italians. . . . Always maintained high standards."[10]

An interview with Paul Grande,[11] a lifelong resident of the North End and an Avellinese barber on North Square for more than fifty years, revealed some interesting comments:

My father first opened the business at the turn-of-the-century. My brother Domenic [see Plate 21] and I joined him as soon as we were old enough. There were many family shops in the North End. Each catered to a regular clientele, made up mostly of *paesani* and people from the nearby buildings. Even though there were many barber shops, we all did a very regular business. We had as many as four barbers at one time. Now there is just my brother and me. Business has really changed. In the old days we were even opened on Sundays. We would first close the shades of course. The men who gathered on North Square and Hanover Street liked to get a shave on Sunday. They didn't go to church much on Sunday, but they wanted to look their best in front of their friends.

Pasquale Verro[12] commented that most of the barbers worked in walking distance of the North End. In Boston, that means, of course, all of Downtown, the West End, and much of the Back Bay. He added:

Many of them had shops in large office buildings and hotels. Others either worked or owned Downtown shops. Americans did not yet consider it in style to go to an Italian barber. It was not considered a profession but more of a lower class job. Our shop on Hanover Street was one of four or five in just one block. We had a regular business. Many members of one family would come. Sicilian dialects and Neapolitan dialects were spoken more often than English. The barber had to speak the dialect of the client to stay in business in the early days. It helped if many of your *paesani* were living in the area.

The network of family barber shops in the North End and environs was certainly not considerably different from the many family-owned and operated shops in other communities. However, the frequent testimony on the role of the extended family and old-world village members in the North End shops is unique. This role still functioned as recently as my childhood days in the early 1950s. My father took me to a barber shop on Friend Street—about a twenty minute walk away from my home. When asked why we went there instead of one of the many shops nearer home, my dad answered, "Domenic is the godfather of my brother. . . . Besides, he gives good haircuts." Searching for a more detailed explanation years later, I found that my paternal grandfather was once an apprentice barber in another shop owned by Domenic's family. My uncle Mario also became a barber there. Both Domenic's family and mine came from the same Italian town—Chiusano San Domenico (about 40 miles from Naples). This type of family network provided employment for its members, and was sustained by others who maintained the kinship.

Two of the most colorful of all the "occupations" listed in the *Directory* were "fruit vendor" and "peddler." Visitors to Boston have long commented on the pushcart trade which has dominated the North End market area since colonial days. These two forms of employment are still readily apparent in the revitalized Dock Square-Quincy Market area, which was mentioned earlier. The *Boston City Directory* revealed a 6.43 percent figure for the fruit vendors in 1899, and a 3.01 percent for that same category in 1929. The "peddler" category reflected a similar 30-year diminution, with a 1.67 percent figure in 1899, and a .645 percent in 1929. I have already described the importance of the Badaracco family to the fruit and vegetable trade in Boston. Alexander Badaracco, the patriarch of the family, was representative of the earliest Italian settlers in the North End in that he was a northern Italian. His son Andrea (see Plate 23) married Rosa Leveroni, a North End Italian "deb," in 1885. By the turn of the century, the family applied its funds to the creation of an undertaking business and a very successful real estate firm. By this time, the fruit business, which has been dominated by enterprising northern Italians, had become the domain of the recently arrived southern Italian peasants.[13]

The "grocery" business was one related field, listed in the *Directory* with a 2.53 percent average for the four sample years. While a few of these developed into large import houses,[14] most of them were of the "ma and pa" variety. Miss Pietrina Maravigna, a retired newspaper columnist, has been a lifetime member of the North End Italian community. She remembered those stores very well, mentioning that Fulton Street had stores such as Pastene's and Musolino's; Richmond Street had Tassinari's; Salem Street had Pappas, and Unity Street had DeVoto's.[15] When asked to describe her family's involvement in the food business in Boston, she said:

You know that we owned the Maravigna Macaroni Company well over seventy years ago. I remember the grocery business well because my older sister and I used to help out with the books years ago. The grocery stores in the North End all had regular customers. People would go to a particular store because it carried their favorite brand of sausage, or something special from the *paese* in the old country. For example, no grocery store would ever attract Avellinese customers if it did not carry *soprasatta* (a sausage made from pig's head) at Eastertime. The Avellinese—and all Neapolitans for that matter—used *soprassata* with goat's cheese to make their Easter meatpie, *pizzagaena*. You remember that the Sicilians used to live together on North Street. Well they had their favorite grocery stores too. I don't remember the names now, but Sicilians used to shop at Dock Square, rather than at the grocery stores along Salem Street, which catered to the Jewish and Neapolitan population at that time.

Pietrina Maravigna's comments were similar to those of Joseph Tassinari, a septuagenarian Genoese member of the North End Community. His family owned "Tassinari Import Foods" at the turn of the century. Both Maravigna and Tassinari agreed that certain grocery stores catered to certain Italians. Mr. Tassinari expressed it in this manner:

Our store which first opened in 1894, would have been the same if you looked at it 30 years later. It was mainly for the Genoese, but, being realistic, we had to appeal to other Italians to stay in business because there just were not enough Genoese in the North End to make our business profitable. We were located on Richmond Street, which bordered on the Sicilian section. Interestingly, the Sicilians went to the open market at Dock Square-Haymarket for most of their groceries. Our customers who were not Genoese came from the

Avellinese section up on North Square. Even when most of the Genoese moved out of the North End in favor of Charlestown, they used to walk over the City Square Bridge on Saturday to do their shopping at our store. One thing you have to remember is that Italians did not go to the nearest store for groceries but went to the store which they knew carried their favorite regional foods.

In April, 1980, an interview with the 86-year-old Avellinese Silvio Iacopucci helped identify other grocery stores as well:

I began helping out at the family store, Totella's on Hanover Street, when I was about 12 years old. Our family has been in the grocery business since my father first came here in the 1880s. You want to know about grocery stores? Well, let me tell you, there were many grocery stores at the beginning of the century. There was Savarese on Hanover Street, Angiullo on Prince Street, Polcari on North Margin Street, Martignetti on Salem Street, DeVoto on Unity Street, Pastene on Fulton Street, Tassinari on Richmond Street, and Pappas on Salem Street. Each store had customers from different places in Italy. I know our store had a lot of *Chiusanesi* (from Chiusano San Domenico, Avellino) customers. This is interesting because our shop was near the Sicilian area, but they shopped at the open market at Dock Square instead of our place. I opened my own grocery store on Fleet Street in 1919; my customers were still mostly *Chiusanesi*.

These comments were in agreement with my overall findings concerning work and purchasing patterns for the North End Italians. The three most frequent responses to the question "Why did you shop for groceries where you did?" were: (1), familial relationship to owner; (2), quality of product from native Italian region; and (3), ability to meet with *paesani* while shopping. The location of the "enclave" did not necessarily seem to be important in selecting the establishment frequented. The "enclave" extended whatever distance necessary to make the "right" grocery store part of the everyday life of these Campanians and Sicilians.

Two occupations almost totally dominated by one Italian "enclave" were "fisherman" and "baker," with the Sicilians of North Street accounting for most of both. These occupations provided regular work for the members of the "enclave" to arrive in the Boston Italian community. In the *Boston City Directory* 1.67 percent of the North End Italian population was listed as "fisherman." Entire families were listed as such.

Most of the earliest "bakeries" began as bread and pizza outlets, only later developing into pastry shops. A 1976 interview with the Avellinese John Plescia,[16] a true master pastry chef since World War I, revealed some insight into the distinctions between Italian ethnic bakeries in the North End:

There has always been an apprenticeship system in this business. One of my teachers in the pastry business was Domenico Carbone, who was the master Sicilian pastry chef in the North End. I have been in the business since World War I, and have provided training to many of the best Italian pastry chefs in Greater Boston. Most of the North End specialties are either Neapolitan, Roman, or Sicilian. The business is always very competitive. Each shop has always drawn its regular customers from *paesani*. By this I mean that Neapolitans and Sicilians usually go to their own shops. One example is that not all-pastry shops make the traditional Neapolitan pastry specialty *Zeppule di San Giuseppe* in March.

John Plescia's mention of Domenico Carbone, who was from Catania, Sicily, reminded me of the many "stories of the old days" I had heard from Mr. Carbone during my own youth, when I lived above his "Etna Pastry Shop" (named after Mt. Etna in his native Catania, Sicily) on Prince Street. He died at the age of 93 in 1969. He was very proud of the fact that he was the first North End baker to make the braided Easter baskets and Sicilian Easter lamb pastry—a skill he eventually taught to most of the North End pastry chefs. A 1980 conversation with his daughter Anna D'Ambrosio, who carried on her father's trade until her own retirement in February, 1980, revealed:

> We had a clientele that went back all the way to the last century. Our shop was the best Sicilian pastry shop in Boston all those years. Look at all the awards and letters over there on the wall (she pointed to a wall filled with autographed photographs from celebrities spanning most of the century). My father told me many times that he made such good quality Sicilian Easter lambs and braided baskets in the beginning that many of the other pastry shops used to buy his, and then resell them at a higher price.

The restaurant business accounted for 1.55 percent of the employment of North End Italians, according to the *Boston City Directory*. This figure requires more analysis than many of the others. The current image of the North End as a quaint place to visit for an occasional Italian dinner is an outgrowth of the increase in tourism to the area in the 1970s. Italians generally did not frequent Italian restaurants. Coffee shops and pizza parlors were the exceptions. Italians listed as restaurant workers in the *Boston City Directory* generally worked in the downtown area of Boston. The *Directory* identified the Parker House Hotel as a major place of employment for North End Italian restaurant workers. The maitre d'hotel in the 1919 *Boston Directory* was identified as a North End Italian. Michael De Marco,[17] who worked in his father's Moon Street and Garden Court Street restaurants just after World War I, said:

> Most of our business was coffee and sandwiches . . . a lunch trade. Many of the men who lived in the North End without their wives came in for an occasional homemade Neapolitan dish. We catered to the Avellinese population that lived in the North Square area. The restaurants were not fancy, but did serve good food. I learned how to cook *cacciatore* when I was a young teenager. That dish was popular. We later opened a pizza shop on Thatcher Street. That became very successful. My father sold the Regina Pizzeria [see Plate 32] after World War II. During the period you're asking about (1900-1930), we lived over our Moon Street restaurant.

The "hotel" business, which employed close to one percent of the labor force, according to the *Directory's* statistics, also reflected the "enclaves." Most of the area hotels which were primarily owned by the Piscopo family, were residence hotels for men who lived in Boston without their families. Names such as Hotel Napoli, Hotel Haymarket, and Hotel Venice, respectively catered to Neapolitans, Sicilians, and northern Italians. Even their names gave the distinct impression that rather than just trying to be continental, they were appealing to a particular subcultural group. Remembering that the North End had a reputation as the "gambling-dance hall-bistro-prostitution" section of the city long before the Italian arrival,[18] and that as far back as April 23, 1851, 92 prostitutes were arrested there in one night, one logical question was what kind of illegal activities were regular attractions at the "Italian hotels" at the turn of the century. Most of the men interviewed had very certain memories of the prostitution activities at the area hotels. They recalled the Sicilian activities at the Hotel Haymarket on Causeway Street and particularly remembered the North Square Hotel Italia, later known as the Hotel Rex. This hotel catered to the Avellinese by 1895. Gambling and prostitution were commonplace there. Most of the girls were Irish in the beginning, attributable to the Irish control of these businesses since the days of their initial settlement in the 1840s. Avellinese gained control of the assorted hotel trades about the time World War I began. My father (see plate 18) remembered that as a little boy of only eight he saw a major brawl in front of the Hotel Rex in North Square over an Avellinese assertion that the Taurasi area of Campania grew larger lemons than anywhere in Sicily. The Sicilian in question took exception, and a stiletto duel ensued. My father was not certain which area did in fact grow larger lemons, but did say that the man from Taurasi won the contest. The mixture of characters was such that Charles Dickens would probably have had enough material for several novels.

It must be stated that while violence and crime were certainly not foreign to the North End, they did not dominate the life of the community. Few individuals made a living as criminals. The type of conflict described above was not part of any "organized"[19] attempt to dominate the community. It was rather an expression of fierce loyalty to one's perceived homeland.

The "George Scigliano Collection" at the University of Minnesota provides a glimpse into both the activity of the "organized crime" element in the community, and the community's response to it. The Neapolitan "Camorra," and the Sicilian "Mafia" were both active in the community in 1900. George Scigliano became a target for the "Camorra's" wrath when, in 1904, he introduced legislation which would have made certain immigrant bank activities illegal in Massachusetts. He worked diligently in the Massachusetts State Legislature to require that immigrant banking funds could not be collected by *padroni* (Italian labor agents), but only by licensed state

Figure 6. 1912 Postal Savings Bank Book belonging to Maria Grazia Cristiano De Marco, paternal grandmother of the author.

banking institutions. Italians regularly sent their life's savings back to the hometown bank in their *paese.* (See figure 6.) The *padroni,* who Scigliano felt were greatly influenced by the "Camorra" and "Mafia," often charged exorbitant rates for these services, and, in some cases, absconded with the funds. This was commonplace not only among Italians. A *Boston Post* article[20] in 1904, identified Hebrew, Polish, and Swedish labor merchants who practiced similar acts of deception. Scigliano's bill exempted steamship companies and state licensed banking institutions. This bill passed in 1904. He then received a death threat[21] from the Neapolitan "Camorra," which was more active in the predominantly Neapolitan North End than the Sicilian "Mafia." The vast majority of Italians were outraged. George Scigliano subsequently formed a vigilance committee, which intended to rid the city of "Italian & Sicilian thugs."[22] Scigliano died mysteriously not long after this incident. The question of whether he was poisoned was never resolved.

The Scigliano affair again illustrated the role of subcultural groups in the life of the North End Italian community. All of the sources available clearly pointed to a Neapolitan organization of criminals preying on their own people. The Sicilian "Mafia," like the Sicilian population of the North End, played a secondary role here. This unfortunate incident also pointed to the role of labor agents in the "employment" process in the North End. The *padrone* system[23] has been widely written about and its merits debated. The North End had two major labor agents during this period. They were Torchia and Company, and Stabile and Company. Both of these firms worked closely with the White Star Shipping Lines, which had weekly direct passenger arrivals to the port of Boston from Naples and Genoa.[24] Most of their contacts, however, were made through the port of New York. These agencies provided Boston factories with Neapolitan and other southern Italian manpower through a network of contacts which extended all the way to villages in southern Italy. Passage and employment was provided in return for a year of employment with the contracting firm. However, the North End community did not prove to be their main focus of activity. Most of the Italians who arrived in Boston through the auspices of these labor agents were given jobs in areas of Maine and Canada.

Anthony Poto, the son of the founder of the Banco Stabile in the North End, provided some illumination on this topic just before his death in 1978. He was in his eighties at the time of the interview. In reply to the charges of exploitation, Mr. Poto defended his family's role as guardians of the welfare of these recent sons and daughters of the *Mezzogiorno:*

> My father provided many services for the immigrants through his bank. We naturally were
> in the business of making money, but did run an honest business. Some of the agents in
> Boston at the time were rather unscrupulous. What would happen was that a business that
> wanted to hire Italians would approach us for assistance. We would make an arrangement

with our contacts in Naples concerning how many men were needed for a particular contract. We always dealt with men only. Since the immigrants needed a job and sponsor to come here, we were happy to provide them with both. We received a commission from the company that hired them. From this we had to pay for the Italians' ship passage, and also pay a commission to the agent in Naples. He then had to pay a commission to the individuals who acted as *padrone* in the local village. Unlike most agents, we did not continue to charge a fee for this service. Instead, we hoped that the Italians would save money at our bank, or have us ship the money to their bank in Italy. The men would also come to us for help when it was time for them to send for their wives or other members of the family. Since many of the Italian men who came here before World War I returned to Italy several times before they either permanently settled here or there, we very often helped with arranging the papers for the return to Italy and back. We sometimes provided help to an individual Italian who needed help finding a job after he had been here for awhile.

One of the things we learned early was that individuals from the same town or region worked best together. Contracts which required large numbers of men, like the Canadian railroad contracts, were usually filled with as many men from the same region as possible. We could count on repeat business only if both the Italians and the contracting companies were satisfied. Not everyone operated this way. Like I said before, many *padrone* and agents for other nationalities were cruel. We stayed in the banking business all these years because we have always run the place with decency.[25]

The *Directory* listed a total of 16 North End residents, who were physicians, for the four sample years, for a .49 percent. Twenty of the thirty-eight practicing physicians[26] in the North End in 1920 were Italians. There were six Italian dentists in the North End as well.

Dr. Frank Leonardi,[27] who had been a lifelong De Marco family friend, was fortunately interviewed six months prior to his death in 1978. An octogenarian, Dr. Leonardi tended to ramble somewhat, but did say:

There were many gifted doctors among the Italians in the old days. The one thing that hurt is that the Greater Boston community never gave our people any credit for producing professionals. The doctors did a lot of valiant work during the Great Flu Epidemic after World War I. When I was in the State Legislature, I worked very hard to make sure there would be a health unit in the North End.

The legal profession was well represented in the North End Italian community. There was George Scigliano,[28] for example, who was a member of the State Legislature at the turn of the century, and became the first Boston Italian to serve on the Common Council in 1902. Attorney Joseph Brogna was appointed to judge in 1927. Joseph De Marco—no relationship—after serving as editor of the *Gazzetta del Massachusetts,* graduated from Harvard Law School in 1924. Names such as Langone, Piemonte, Leveroni, Forte, Mondello, and others have been associated with the legal profession in the community[29] since the late nineteenth century.

Thus far my research has established that Italians preferred working with other Italians from the same province or region. Obviously, more extensive study is required in the very important area of subcultural dominance of any specific area of employment. One avenue of study, however, which has recently enjoyed growing interest on the part of the scholars is that of the "immigrant women in the labor force."[30]

The *Boston City Directory* listed very few women as either residents or employed individuals for the four sample years, with only a 5.21 percent average in both categories out of all individuals sampled. Joseph Cassia, who had returned to Italy twice before permanently settling here, gave a representative explanation for this when he said that wives and girlfriends were back in the *paese*. He felt that most of the men who worked here had but one ambition—to make enough money to live in the old village with dignity. He noticed that fewer and fewer individuals returned to Italy after World War I. By that time, he observed, many women from Italy had come to the North End. In effect, he was saying that the North End began to feel like home because it began to resemble the old-world villages. "Enclaves" had made the perpetuation of *la via vecchia* possible.

The two single greatest employers of women in the North End were the "confectionary" and "tailor/seamstress" industries. During the period prior to the Great Depression of the 1930s, the candy factories were scattered throughout the entire area which surrounds the North End residential section. Luisa Digiustini, while commenting on the employment of Abruzzesi women, said about the candy companies:

> These companies were good employers for the women because they had ideal working schedules, and did not require any special skill or training in the beginning. A woman started out in the boxing sections. They were paid by the box, so they could work as many hours as they wanted. They did not need any schooling for the work. You have to remember that most of the women were illiterate in the beginning. The men were the ones that had the education. If a woman worked hard, and showed some promise, she would eventually work up to becoming a chocolate dipper. . . . Sicilian women worked far more regularly than any other group of Italians. I don't know why, but it's true. Abruzzesi women did not work outside the home at all. Their husbands wouldn't allow it.

Palmy and Eleanor Barassi, who were supervisors at the William Schrafft's Confectionary Company for more than a quarter of a century, commented that even since World War II, Italian women in their factory have come to work in groups or clusters. They generally spoke a dialect, and tried to work together in one boxing area of the plant. "It is not uncommon even today for entire families of Italian immigrant women not to come to work on a given day. One of them may get sick, and the others don't go because they tend to associate relatively exclusively among themselves."

The *Boston Directory* rarely listed any employment for Italian women in all four sample years. The North End confectionary companies, however, accounted for almost 40 percent of all the employment *listed* for women. Of all Italians sampled (both men and women), 3.31 percent were involved in the confectionary trade. More than half of these (58.1 percent) were women.

The tailor/seamstress category was the single greatest employer of Italian women. As the wool manufacturing center of the world from the late nineteenth century through World War II, Boston employed thousands of individuals in the garment industry. Maria Cassia, (see Plates 35-38) who worked as a seamstress for well over 50 years, remembers the period just after World War I:

> After my husband returned from the war, I continued to work as a stitcher at a place on Stuart Street. We got paid by the number of pieces we stitched. I worked a lot faster in those days than I can do now. We didn't have any immediate family living in Boston yet at that time, but we did have some *compari*. They used to work with my husband on his construction jobs, and the wives would go to work in the clothing factory together. Some of the factories had a place where the babies would be taken care of so we could work inside. My son Sammy used to go to work with me when he was a little baby. I worked those years because my husband and I wanted to buy a house with some land. We eventually saved enough money to buy a house in Revere, near some of our *paesani*. As you can see, we have a large garden in the back where we grow tomatoes, peppers, colrabbi, and a lot of other things. That didn't come till after the period you're asking about, though. About the factory, I remember that the Italians, Jews, and Irish always sat in separate places. Most of the Italians there were Sicilians. I used to go to work with my *compare*. If either one of us got sick, the other one didn't go to work because we didn't want to go alone. I was very good as a seamstress, and never wanted to become a cutter. They very rarely made Italians fabric cutters, anyway. They were usually Jewish men. When I retired a little more than twenty years ago, they had a nice party for me.

The number of women involved in the garment industry in Boston was significant. North End Italian women were employed more in this trade than in any other. The *Boston City Directory*, though remarkably silent about Italian women, does list the garment trade with the greatest percentage of those employed (51.3 percent). Unfortunately, however, there is no way to accurately determine just how many women were involved in that business. Many women worked at home, by the piece, and never declared any income.

It is not fair, of course, to characterize all North End Italian women of the period as individuals with relatively menial forms of employment. There were professionals numbered among their ranks as well; for example, Doctors Luisa Leveroni and Rose Jannini, who were born in Boston and the first Italian women doctors in New England, resided in the community. So too did Dr. Fenecia Leonardi,[31] a North End-born dentist. Several North End women even achieved fame internationally, due to their stage performances. The two most notable examples were Elvira Leveroni (see Plate 24) and Louise

Badaracco, both of whom sang leading roles with the San Carlo Opera Company in Naples, as well as the Boston and Metropolitan Opera Companies in the United States.[32] However, these were not representative of the vast majority of Italian women who got married, reared children, and carried on traditional roles within the framework of *la famiglia*.

My research points to a greater number of women employed than the records show. Some were professional. Most were not. While it is true that the majority of Italian women who worked held rather low paying positions, it is equally true that the greatest number of North End Italian women worked full-time at being homemakers. Most men would have it no other way. This does not mean that the women did not agree with the decision. They valued the importance of the tenets of *la via vecchia* at least as much as their husbands. With few exceptions, this did not allow for a confusion of family roles. Those that did work, especially if married with children, brought their familial network of relationships with them to the place of employment.

This chapter has shown that Italians worked at a variety of jobs to sustain their families, and managed within the employment framework to maintain many of the old-world values they brought to Boston from their Italian villages. As had been the case in their enclaves, marriage patterns, and religious experiences, *la via vecchia* was nurtured in the North End working environment.

Plate 18. William De Marco, Sr., father of the author, age
          seven years, on the roof of his Moon Street
          apartment, 1927

Plate 19. Paternal grandparents of author: Maria Grazia and
Giuseppe De Marco, with children (*l.* to *r.*) Mario, Gene,
Michael, and Fiore. Photo was taken at Moon Street
residence in 1916.

Plate 20. Gaetano Grande (right), with his brother, Riccardo. Gaetano owned a "Neapolitan barber shop" on North Square, from 1906 until his death in 1972. This photo was taken in 1910, when he was 26 years old.

Plate 21. Domenic Grande on a pony in front of his father's
North Square barber shop, 1925

Plate 22. Domenic Grande's First Communion photo, taken at the Frank Barassi Studio, Prince Street, North End of Boston, 1928

Plate 23. Andrea Badaracco, son of Alessandro Badaracco, one of
Boston's first Italian entrepreneurs. Andrea was a
successful real estate broker, and undertaker. He also
served as a member of the Massachusetts Legislature.
Photo taken in 1910.

Plate 24. Elvira Leveroni, a member of the prominent family of the
same name, in a press photo dated 1913. She was a
leading soprano with the San Carlo, Boston, and
Metropolitan Opera Companies prior to World War I.

Plate 25.   James Sablone, dressed in uniform of Italian
Army, after he returned to Italy to fight in World
War I. Photo taken in 1915.

Plate 26. Photo of James Sablone taken at the Frank
Barassi Studios, Prince Street, North End of
Boston, 1919.

Plate 27. James Sablone during last
days of bachelorhood

Plate 28. James Sablone with young
bride Tillie, while on winter
outing. Photo taken in 1928.

Plate 29. Foreman James Sablone
          inspecting shingles for new
          project, 1928.

Plate 30.   Tillie Sablone with father and family, 1916.

Plate 31. Joseph Cassia with wife
Maria, 1928.

Plate 32. Joseph De Marco, left, author's paternal
grandfather, with daughter Helena, at family-
owned Regina Pizzeria at end of prohibition, 1933.

Plate 33. Joseph Cassia in Gardner, Mass., 1926. He was working as a furniture maker at this time.

Plate 34. Parents and younger sisters of Joseph Cassia,
taken in Solarino, Sicily, 1922.

Plate 35. Maria Cassia (on right) with mother and family in Solarino, Sicily, 1903.

Plate 36. Formal portrait of newlywed Maria Cassia, taken
in Frank Barassi Studios, Prince Street, North
End of Boston, 1916.

Plate 37. Mother and son owners of Maverick Mill, East Boston, babysitting for Maria Cassia, who, like many other Sicilian women, worked in their plant. The child is Joseph Cassia, Jr., and the photo was taken in 1923.

Plate 38. Maria Cassia on Retirement Day, September, 1967. This photo was taken at the Sherman Classics Sportswear Company, Boston.

Conclusion

The North End of Boston has been home to thousands of individuals from the Italian peninsula for a century now. Most of the earliest of these settlers were from Genoa and northern Italy, but by the dawn of the twentieth century, new immigrants from the *Mezzogiorno* greatly outnumbered their North Italian counterparts. At least until 1930, which is the last year of my study, these sons and daughters mostly from the *Mezzogiorno* identified with their ancestral habitat with exclusive provincial loyalty. A complex network of relationships, which relied heavily on both the nuclear and extended family for survival in the old-world, was transplanted in the North End of Boston by the late nineteenth century. This network of relationships, which had been molded by centuries of man-made and natural disasters, was particularly reflected in the subcultural enclaves which became new Italian villages in the heart of Boston.

The North End Italian enclaves were initially inhabited by Genoese and other northern Italian immigrants in the 1870s and 1880s. As the Italian subcultural population of the North End increased in subsequent decades, these enclaves increased both in size and number. Throughout the entire period under study here, distinct subcultural enclaves were the norm, and, though frequently unnoticed by contemporary non-Italian government officials such as census takers, their existence was clearly a part of the Italian subculture in the community. Individual tenement blocks were primarily occupied by individuals from any one of four distinct regions of Italy: Campania, Sicily, Abruzzi, and Genoa. The overwhelming presence of individuals from Avellino in Campania was particularly manifest in the housing patterns, as was the existence of individuals from Sicily. The Abruzzesi "enclaves" were considerably smaller, and the Genoese enclaves all but disappeared by the end of the period studied. While the North End had been home for a diversity of ethnic groups in the first years of my study, the ever-increasing Italian "enclaves," and the existence of more desirable neighborhoods forced out non-Italian residents by World War I.

The retention of old-world values was manifest in more than just housing patterns. The community's residents from the *Mezzogiorno* displayed a marked propensity to marry individuals from their native southern Italian villages throughout the entire period studied. Church marriage records clearly show that not only did they average five weddings per church every week from 1890 to 1930 but also close to 90 percent of these weddings were between individuals from the same Italian region. In more than half of these instances, marriages were between individuals from the same Italian villages. This tendency to marry individuals from the same village and region was as strong at the end of the period studied as in the beginning, though the number of marriages had diminished by 1930.

Church records for the two Italian churches proved to be valuable in other areas of study as well. The history of the formation of both Saint Leonard of Port Maurice and Sacred Heart Italian Churches reflect the tensions these immigrants experienced at the hands of the Irish Catholic community, but these tensions were no more pronounced than the inner turmoil created within the "Italian" community by centuries-old mistrust of individuals from the "wrong" Italian regions. Each of these two Roman Catholic houses of worship served distinctly different Italian subcultures, even though they were located only one short block apart. Baptismal records in each church not only showed that they averaged close to twenty baptisms apiece each week for every year from 1890 to 1930 but that distinctly different villages within similar provinces and regions were also represented in their respective Sacramental Files. Even the history of religious societies, which were most often located at either of these churches in the beginning, reflects that members associated with individuals from their own respective villages most frequently, wherever and whenever this was possible.

The employment statistics, though not as conclusive as the church records, did provide some verification of the existence of old-world values. The frequency of individuals with the same name working at the same job was quite high in my sample of the *Boston City Directory*. Oral testimony taken from more than 50 residents of the community, with a median age of 69.4 years, revealed that southern Italians did generally work with other southern Italians from the same province or region, wherever possible. The purchasing patterns of both goods and services were most often determined by some relationship with the old-world village as well.

Some readers may take exception with the fact that I do not provide a chronological study of one of the most "colorful" ethnic communities in the United States. This is a valid point, of course, but I felt that Anna Martellone's work, which is less than ten years old, is an adequate chronological study of the North End during the same time period I analyzed. My concern here was rather one of perspective, and not chronology. The community has been viewed by nonresidents with curiosity turned amazement; it has never really been explained from the perspective of the residents themselves.

The North End "Italian" community of 1981 only vaguely reflects the community of a century ago. It has changed as a result of urban renewal, and because the migration which provided its enclaves with new sons and daughters of the *Mezzogiorno* has long since ceased. What has been presented in these pages has been an attempt to explore the quality of life in a rapidly changing urban community while it remains within the living memory of the present residents. Many of those interviewed for this work died before its completion. The "Italian" community is itself yielding to entrepreneurial pressures which makes it seem most unlikely that it will exist as a living ethnic neighborhood twenty years hence.

What is contained in these pages is a view of one of America's most fascinating ethnic neighborhoods, as perceived by the residents themselves. I hope that this work will encourage similar studies, which recognize that ethnic neighborhoods are social laboratories, and as such, contain countless stories worth telling.

Appendix

Table A1. Oral Interviews

Name	Month/Day	Year	Approximate Age
Frank Barassi	9/4	1975	80
Arthur Bruno	7/21	1976	60
Bianca Bruno	4/17, 6/3	1965	80
Emilio Buccelli	7/18	1974	60
Domenico Carbone	passim	1969	93
Johanna Cassia	3/21, 4/24	1976	55
Joseph Cassia	8/7, 9/18	1977	85
Maria Cassia	8/7, 9/18	1977	80
Santo Cassia	3/21, 4/24	1976	60
Anna D'Ambrosio	11/14	1977	60
Angie D'Amelio	10/4	1977	60
Christoforo D'Amelio	9/27	1975	85
Gene DeMarco	11/5, 12/7	1976	65
Jennie DeMarco	11/5, 12/7	1976	60
Margaret DeMarco	passim	1976-1980	55
Maria Grazia DeMarco	1/18, 4/7	1965	80
Michael DeMarco	11/18	1976	75
William DeMarco, Sr.	passim	1976-1979	59
Luisa Digiustini	11/14	1977	60
Caesar Donnaruma	4/2, 7/9	1976	75
Phyllis Donnaruma	4/2, 7/9	1976	60
Charles Falco	3/1	1978	60
Rev. Bede Ferrara	2/11	1979	55
Nelson Florio	8/17	1977	65
Phyllis Florio	8/17	1977	65
Domenic Grande	11/20	1979	60
Gaetano Grande	9/11	1972	88
Paul Grande	3/14, 9/21	1977	65
Samuel Gurwitz	10/30	1979	70
Silvio Iacopucci	4/5	1980	86
Rev. Joseph Invernizzi	11/7	1977	55
Frederic Langone	5/7	1977	55
Dr. Frank Leonardi	2/21, 7/21	1977	80
Pietrina Maravigna	3/17, 4/21	1976	65
Rev. Pio Parolin	8/23	1961	90
Rev. Remigio Pigato	7/22, 7/29	1976	75
Elvira Plescia	4/29	1976	75
John Plescia	4/29	1976	75
Ada Poto	8/30	1979	75
Anthony Poto	8/4	1977	85
James Sablone	5/18, 5/27	1975	80
Tillie Sablone	5/18, 5/27	1975	70
John Sala	8/19	1977	65
Helen Sala	1/19	1979	55
Louis Salerno	7/13, 9/21	1976	60
Rev. Louis Savio	8/18	1976	60
Dr. Gaetano Sciacca	2/14, 5/22	1977	55
Alfredo Tassinari	8/14	1977	103
Joseph Tassinari	9/18	1979	70
Fr. Ubaldus	12/16	1979	80
Pasquale Verro	8/4	1977	65
Pat Voto	12/13	1976	65
Rev. Hillary Zanon	8/14, 11/3	1978	65

Table A2.   North End Italian Societies in 1910

Name	Year of Founding	Area of Italy	Church Affiliation	Members
*Mutuo Coccorso	1868	Genoa	+SL	35
Italiana Colombo	1869	Genoa	SL	50
*San Marco	1884	Genoa	+SH	400
Maria Ss. Ausiliatrice	1889	Genoa	SH	45
Bersaglieri	1891	Mixed [North]	SH	75
Ligure	1894	Genoa	SH	?
Maria Ss. Ausiliatrice	1894	Avellino	SL	140
San Ciriaco	1896	Ancona	SH	125
Conte di Torino	1897	Piedmont	SH	150
*Maria Ss.Buon Consiglio	1900	Avellino	SH	70
Di Montefalcione	1900	Avellino	SH	?
*San Antonio	1900	Mixed [South]	SL	100
San Giovanni di Messina	1902	Messina	SL	60
San Gaetano	1902	Naples	SH	80
San Michele di Serino	1902	Avellino	SH	200
Apice di Benevento	1903	Benevento	?	70
S. Maria delle Grazie	1903	Avellino	SH	100
S. Tomaso d"Aquino	1903	Naples	?	80
Carabinieri	1903	Mixed	?	42
A. Vespucci	1903	Florence	SH	110
San Giuseppe di Lapio	1903	Avellino	?	85
Chiusano San Domenico	1904	Avellino	SH	100
Sangue e Protezione di Gesu'	1904	Sicily	SL	?
Societa' di Montemarano	1904	Avellino	?	90
San Feliciano	1904	Avellino	?	325
*San Rocco	1904	Naples	SH	100
Imera	1905	Palermo	?	?
Carpignano	1906	Puglia	?	?
Etna Club	1906	Catania	SL	90
S.Maria Grazie di Paterno Sila	1906	Calabria	?	82
*Montevergine	1906	Avellino	SH	70
Pompeii	1906	Naples	SH	60
San Pietro di Roma	1906	Rome	SH	35
Garibaldi	1907	Mixed [North]	?	56
Vittorio Emanuele	1907	Piedmont	?	40
Fratellanza Siciliana	1907	Sicily	?	250
Taurasi	1907	Avellino	SH	90
S. Teodoro	1907	Abruzzi	SL	40
Stella della Calabria	1907	Cosenza	?	60

(Based on statements and records of North End Italian Clergy,
testimony of residents, and Anna Martellone, Una Little Italy
nell'Atene d'America,[Napoli: Guida Editori, 1973], pp.577-580.)

*Still in existence in 1980.

+SL=Saint Leonard of Port Maurice Church
SH=Sacred Heart Italian Church

Table A3. North End Italian Surnames Sampled for Employment Data*

Aicardi	Cicero	DiBello	Gregori
Albertini	Cogliano	DiBenedetto	Gribitosi
Alioto	Collelo	DiBilio	Guinasso
Anzalone	Colucci	DiBlasi	Guttadauro
Bagigalupo	Coluci	DiCarlo	Iacono
Baglio	Conaci	DiCologero	Iacopucci
Baratta	Corado	DiFranzo	Iacoviello
Barbero	Corigliano	DiGiacomo	Ianetta
Barasso	Correia	DiGirolamo	Iannacone
Baretta	Corsiglia	DiMarco	Iannetta
Basile	Corso	DiMaria	Iannetti
Basillio	Costa	DiMattero	Imperato
Basso	Costanza	DiMattia	Indelicato
Battaglia	Cotello	DiMauro	Iorio
Beatrice	Cristiano	DiPaolo	Ippolito
Belmonte	Cristofaro	DiPerri	Labadini
Benedetto	D'Agostino	DiPesa	Lafauci
Bernardi	D'Amato	Falco	Lamarca
Bernazzini	D'Amico	Falcone	Lamartini
Biondi	D'Angelo	Fedele	Langone
Bionelli	DaPrato	Federico	Lanzetta
Bioni	DeAngelis	Ferrara	Lanzilli
Bocchino	DeCarlo	Ferrarri	Lanzillo
Borgatti	DeCicco	Ferrarro	Laporta
Borosco	DeCristofano	Ferretti	LaRosa
Bova	DeCristofaro	Ferrullo	Latorella
Bravo	DeCristoforo	Ficariello	Lazzaro
Brigandi	DeFelice	Ficchiello	Lentini
Brignoli	DeFeo	Fiore	Lentino
Brindisi	DeFerari	Fiorella	Leonardi
Bruno	DeFerrari	Fiorentino	Leone
Caggiano	DeFilippo	Fiorenza	Lepore
Camellio	DeFrancesco	Fioretti	Leverone
Cangiano	DeGeronimo	Fiorillo	Lombardi
Capello	DeGiorgio	Fiorine	Lombardo
Caputo	DeGregorio	Foppiano	Longo
Capuccio	DeLeo	Franco	Lopato
Carbone	DeLucca	Frasca	LoPilato
Caruso	DeLucia	Furio	Lopresti
Carvelli	DelVecchio	Fusco	Maffa
Casassa	DeMaggio	Gaeta	Maffei
Casetta	DeMarchi	Galassi	Maffeo
Castaldo	DeMarco	Gallo	Manganiello
Catalano	DeMaria	Gallucci	Mangano
Cataldo	DeMattero	Gallucio	Mangiacomo
Catalfano	DeMattia	Gardella	Marchetti
Cavagnaro	DePasquale	Giordano	Marchione
Cavalli	DePietro	Giovino	Marchisio
Chiesa	DeRosa	Gorini	Marco
Christiana	DeSimone	Gracia	Marini
Ciambelli	DeStefano	Granara	Marino
Ciampa	DeVincenzo	Gravelese	Marrotta
Ciccolo	DeVito	Gravellesi	Martignetti

Table A3. North End Italian Surnames Sampled for Employment Data
(Continued)

Martini
Martino
Masucco
Matarazzo
Mazza
Mazzarella
Mazzei
Mercatante
Messina
Minichiello
Muollo
Musto
Napoli
Napolitano
Nardone
Nazzaro
Negro
Nicoletti
Nunzio
Nutale
Nutali
Orlandi
Orlando
Pagliuca
Palazzolo
Palermo
Palladino
Palma
Palinieri
Palumbo
Parisi
Pasco
Pascucci
Pasqua
Patroni
Pellegrino
Pelosi
Penta
Porcella

Porcello
Prico
Puleo
Puopolo
Reppucci
Ricci
Riccio
Rizzo
Rocco
Romano
Rosetta
Rosetti
Rossi
Rosso
Ruggiero
Russo
Sacco
Salerno
Santosuosso
Sarni
Sarno
Sergi
Severino
Sferazzo
Simonelli
Solari
Spinali
Spinelli
Terraciano
Trabucco
Valente
Valenti
Valeri
Visconte
Vitale
Volpe
Zarella
Zuccaro

*See *Boston City Directory,* 1899, 1909, 1919, 1929.

Table A4. Companies Employing North End Italians in 1909*

Bottling and Canning Companies

    Colonial Can Co., 120 Milk St., Boston
    Elk Flint Co., 111 North St., Boston
    Hilliard Brothers, 387 Atlantic Ave., Boston
    Chas. McNally Tin Can Mfr., 44 India St., Somerville

Confectionary Companies

    Aldrich & Smith Mfg., 21 Portland St., Boston
    W. Baker & Co., Ltd., 45 Broad St., Boston
    F.L.Daggett, Inc., 33-36 Lewis Wharf, Boston
    H.D.Foss & Co., 112 Canal St., Boston
    Hazen Confectionary Co., 119-127 State St., Boston
    H.A.Johnson Bakers & Confectioners, 221-227 State St., Boston
    Walter Lowney Co., 486 Hanover St., Boston
    New England Confectionary Co., 253 Summer St., Boston
    Russell & Co., Confectioners, 253 Norfolk St., Cambridge
    Samoset Chocolates Co., 60 Commerce St., Boston
    Wm. F. Schrafft Co., 16 Charlestown Bridge, Boston

Construction Companies

    Aberthaw Construction Co., 6 Beacon St., Boston
    Michael Dello-Russo Contractors, 16 North Sq., Boston
    Horton & Hemenway, Builders, 683 Atlantic Ave., Boston
    W.F.Kearns Co., 161 Devonshire, Boston

Food & Liquor Import Companies

    Italian-American Wine Co., 204 Hanover St., Boston
    P.Pastene, Food Importers, 69-75 Fulton St., Boston
    John Scaroni Italian Groceries Co., 98 Cross St., Boston
    Spinelli, Capone & Co., Liquor Importers, Boston
    V. Tassinari & Co., Food Importers, 102 Cross St., Boston
    P. Terrile Italian Food Importers, 198-200 Commercial St., Boston

Hotels

    Hotel Haymarket, Causeway St., Boston
    Hotel Marliave, 11 Bosworth St., Boston
    Hotel Napoli, 84-96 Friend St., Boston
    Parker House, 60 School St., Boston
    Hotel Piscopo, 32 Fleet St., Boston
    Hotel Rome, 200 North St., Boston
    Hotel Venice, 181 Hanover St., Boston

*See *Boston City Directory*, 1909 Edition.

Table A4. Companies Employing North End Italians in 1909 *(Continued)*

Masonry Companies

    J.Harrington Granite & Marble Works,52 First St., Cambridge
    Kavanagh Bros. Marble & Granite Monument Co., Quincy
    Levis Marble Mosaic Co., 975 Mass. Ave.,Boston
    Mass. Broken Stone Co., 235 Franklin St., Boston
    Mount Hope Quarry Co., 31 State St., Boston
    New England Marble Mosaic Co-Operative Co., 147 Orleans St.,E.Boston
    Union Soapstone Co., 14 Marshall St., Boston

Metalwork Companies

    Berger Metal Ceilings Mfg. Co.,286 Devonshire St., Boston
    J.B. Ely Tin & Sheet Iron Co., 74 North St., Boston
    Hennessey Brass Works, 54 High St., Boston
    Hercules Iron and Supply Co., 427-445 Commercial St., Boston
    Geo. W. Herrick Iron & Metal Co., 47-49 Broad St., Boston
    Holt, Shattuck Machinery & Tools Co., 45 N. Washington St., Boston
    Fred A. Houdlette Iron & Steel Co., 93 Broad St., Boston
    Keighley Metal Ceiling & Roofing Co., 514-516 Atlantic Ave., Boston
    Kennear & Gager Steel Ceiling Mfg., Co., 125 Broad St.,Boston
    McGann & Sons, Brassfounders, 104-106 Portland St., Boston

Miscellaneous

    Alles & Fisher Cigar Makers, 34 Cambridge St., Boston
    Durable Wire Rope Co., 26-30 Atlantic Ave., Boston
    Haymarket Sq. Tile & Fireplace Co., 26 N. Washington St., Boston
    J.A.Langone, Undertakers, 19 Prince St., Boston
    J.Manzo & Co., 252 Friend St., Boston
    Porcella & Granara, Undertakers, 10 N. Bennett St., Boston

Restaurants

    Cafe Marliave, 11 Bosworth St., Boston
    Leverone & Porcella, 123 North St., Boston
    (No Name),33 North Sq., Boston
       "   ,225 North St., Boston
       "   ,1½ Garden Crt. St., Boston
       "   ,172 North St., Boston
    Parker House Restaurant, 60 School St., Boston
    Ponticelli & Palumbo, 12 Parmenter St., Boston

Table A4. Companies Employing North End Italians in 1909 *(Continued)*

Shoe Companies

Clark-Hutchinson Boot & Shoe Co., 111-115 Federal St., Boston
Cummings Sole Co., 406 Washington St., Boston
Hamilton Brown Shoe Co., 604-610 Atlantic Ave., Boston
Kelley Shoe Findings Co., 200 Congress St., Boston
Kistler Lesh & Co., Tanners, 597 Atlantic Ave., Boston
Winch Bros., Shoe Mfrs., 580 Atlantic Ave., Boston

Textile Companies

Amory, Browne & Co., Commission Merchants, 48 Franklin St., Boston
Catlin & Co., Commission Merchants, 345 Broadway, Boston
Faulkner Page, Commission Merchants, 91 Bedford St., Boston
Fearing Whiton & Co., Commission Merchants, 655 Atlantic Ave., Boston
Frost Ladies Furnighings Mfg.Co., 551 Tremont St., Boston
Thos. Hooper Shirt Mfr., 277 Dartmouth St., Boston
Thos. Hooper Shirt Mrf., 31 West St., Boston
Harding,Whitman & Co.,Commission Merchants,78 Chauncey St., Boston
Howe & Howe, Shirt Mfr., 71 Bromfield St., Boston
Lawrence & Co., Commission Merchants, 89 Franklin St., Boston
Linen Thread Co., 575-577 Atlantic Ave., Boston
Lowe & Co., Woolens Mfr., 100 Chauncey St., Boston
McKenney, Field & Woodman, Commission Merchants,56 Franklin, Boston
Parker, Wilder & Co.,Commission Merchants, 4 Winthrop Sq., Boston
Smith,Hagg & Co.,Commission Merchants, 144 Essex St., Boston
Warren & Blanchard Woolens, 70 Essex St., Boston
Wilson, Larrabbee & Co., Importers &Jobbers, 27 Bedford St., Boston

Woodwork Companies

Ed. Holden Woodware Co., 13 Dock Sq., Boston
Irving & Casson Cabinetmakers, 150 Boylston St., Boston

Notes

Preface

1. For a description of the "quality of life" in the North End prior to the Italian settlement, see George Weston, Jr., *Boston Ways, High, By, and Folk* (Boston: Beacon Press, 1974); Paula Todisco, *Boston's First Neighborhood: The North End* (Boston: Boston Public Library Press, 1976); John Galvin, "Boston's First Irish Cop" *Boston Magazine* 67 n. 3 (March, 1975); Annie Thwing, *The Crooked and Narrow Streets of Boston* (Boston: Marshall Jones Company, 1920); and Oscar Handlin, *Boston's Immigrants* (Cambridge; Harvard University Press, 1941). Robert A. Woods, *Americans in Process* (Boston: Houghton Mifflin, 1903), is the classic work on the Italian settlement. Walter Firey, *Land Use in Central Boston* (New York: Greenwood Press, 1968), is a more recent work on the same topic.

2. Professor Serpe was restating in 1958 what Robert Woods had written more than 50 years earlier in his highly respected study *Americans in Process,* in a chapter entitled "The City Slum."

3. See Robert E. Park and Herbert A. Miller, *Old World Traits Transplanted* (New York: Harper & Brothers, Inc., 1921), pp. 95, 146-159; Leonard Covello, "The Social Background of the Italian-American School Child" (Ph.D. Dissertation, Columbia University, 1941), pp. 442-44; and *The Heart is the Teacher* (New York: McGraw Hill Book Company, Inc., 1958), p. 22.

4. Jacob Riis, "Out of Mulberry Street: Stories of Tenement Life in New York City," *The Century,* 1898, p. 19.

5. G. Schiro, *Americans by Choice: History of Italians in Utica* (Utica: Griffith, 1940), pp. 9, 108-14.

6. F.A. Ianni, "The Acculturation of the Italo-Americans in Norristown, Pennsylvania: 1900-1950" (Ph.D. Dissertation, Pennsylvania State College, 1952), pp. 36-37; and George F. Huganir, "Process and Adaptation to Factory and Community Change" (Ph.D. Dissertation, University of Pennsylvania, 1958), p. 273.

7. Charles W. Churchill, "The Italians of Newark" (Ph.D. Dissertation, New York University, 1942), p. 43.

8. Irvin L. Child, *Italian or American? The Second Generation in Conflict* (New Haven: Yale University Press, 1943), p. 79; Jerome K. Meyers, "The Differential Time Factor in Assimilation: A Study of Aspects and Processes of Assimilation Among the Italians of New Haven" (Ph.D. Dissertation, Yale University, 1949) and *Their Growth and Characteristics* (Hartford: Connecticut State Department of Education, 1938), pp. 26-27.

9.   Walter H. Sangree, "Mel Hyblaeum: A Study of the People of Middletown of Sicilian Origin" (Master's Thesis, Wesleyan University, 1952), p. 1.

10. *Comitato Coloniale per il Congresso degl'Italiani all'Estero, Stato del Connecticut* (Stamford: Società Italiana di Stamford, 1908), pp. 20-25.

11. Charles W. Coulter, *The Italians of Cleveland* (Cleveland: Mayor's Advisory War Committee, 1919), pp. 10-13.

12. George LaPiana, *The Italians of Milwaukee* (Milwaukee: Wisconsin Associated Charities, 1915), p. 5.

13. Robert E. Park and Herbert A. Miller, *Old World Traits Transplanted* (New York: Harper and Brothers, Inc., 1921), p. 42.

14. Amos H. Hawley, "Dispersion versus Segregation: Apropos of a Solution of Race Problems," Paper of the Michigan Academy of Science, Arts, and Letters 30 (1944), p. 668.

15. Oscar Handlin, "Immigration in American Life: A Reappraisal," in Henry S. Commager (ed.) *Immigration in American History: Essays in Honor of Theodore C. Blegen* (Minneapolis: University of Minnesota Press, 1961). p. 13. John Briggs, *An Italian Passage* (New Haven: Yale University Press, 1978), applied this theory to the cities of Utica, Rochester, and Syracuse, New York. Virginia Yans-McLaughlin, *Family and Community* (Ithaca: Cornell University Press, 1977), analyzed the structure of the Italian family in Buffalo, drawing similar conclusions.

16. John S. MacDonald and Leatrice D. MacDonald, "Urbanization, Ethnic Groups, and Social Segmentation," *Social Research* 29 (Winter, 1962), p. 434.

17. Herbert J. Gans, *The Urban Villagers* (New York: The Free Press, 1962), p. 210.

18. Anna Martellone's *Una Little Italy nell'Atena d'America* (Napoli: Guida Editori, 1973), is a chronological history of the North End Italian community, from 1880 to 1920. This work is presently available only in Italian.

Chapter 1

1.   See Francis X. Femminella, *Ethnicity and Ego-Identity* (Ph.D. Dissertation, New York University, 1968), for a detailed application of Eric Erikson's concept of "ego-identity" to the Italian perception of its own culture. In 1976, Professor Femminella collaborated with Jill S. Quadagno in "The Italian American Family," *Ethnic Families in America: Patterns and Variations*, Mindel and Habrestein, eds. (New York: Elsevier Co.), pointing out that the Italian immigrant only assumed an Italian ethnic identity after he arrived in America, and most importantly, only in relationship to non-Italians. Within the Italian community in America, the sense of the family and regional loyalty remained all-important.

2.   Phyllis Williams, *South Italian Folkways in Europe and America* (New Haven: Yale University Press, 1938). Written as a social worker's handbook for the New Haven, Connecticut community, it is a classic work on the subject.

3.   See Leonard Covello, *The Social Background of the Italo-American School Child* (Leider, Netherlands: E.J. Brill, 1967), pp. 23-33; Joseph Lopreato, *Peasants No More* (San Francisco: Chandler, 1970), p. 25; Luciano J. Iorizzo and Salvatore Mondello, *The Italian Americans* (New York: Twayne, 1971), *passim;* Andrew Rolle, *The American Italians* (Belmont, California: Wadsworth, 1972), p. 112; Virginia Yans-McLaughlin, *Family and Community* (Ithaca: Cornell University Press, 1977), pp. 25-55, *passim.*

4. Francis X. Femminella and Jill S. Quadagno, "The Italian American Family," *Ethnic Families in America: Patterns and Variations,* p. 65.

5. For an analysis of the patriarchal-matriarchal system in southern Italy, see Francis X. Femminella, "Patriarchy? Matriarchy? Or Something Else Again?: Authority in the Italian-American Family," *Marriage and the Family,* Barash and Scourby, eds. (New York: Random House, 1970). Richard Gambino, *Blood of my Blood* (New York: Doubleday, 1974), p. 26, briefly discusses the same question.

6. Femminella and Quadagno, "The Italian American Family," p. 65.

7. Gambino, *Blood of My Blood,* p. 225, describes *ben educato* in depth.

8. The importance of *la famiglia* and *campanilismo* is widely recognized. Some of the more detailed works dealing with the subject are Phyllis H. Williams, *South Italian Folkways in Europe and America,* pp. 73-106; Rudolph J. Vecoli, "Contadini in Chicago: A Critique of *The Uprooted," Journal of American History* LI (December, 1964), pp. 404-17; Gambino, *Blood of My Blood,* pp. 1-41.

9. Rudolph J. Vecoli, "Contadini in Chicago: A Critique of *The Uprooted," Journal of American History,* pp. 404-17.

10. Ignazio Silone, *Fontamara* (New York: H. Smith and R. Haas, 1934), p. XVIII.

11. Margaret Carlyle, *The Awakening of Southern Italy* (New York: Oxford University Press, 1962), p. 13.

12. See chapter 2 for a description of Boston's North End and its Italian "enclaves."

13. William Roscoe Thayer's two volume *The Dawn of Italian Independence* (Boston: Houghton Mifflin, 1893), and George MaCauley Trevelyan's trilogy *Garibaldi* (New York: Longman's Green, 1909), are major early works on the topic.

14. The best work in English on the subject is Edward E. Y. Hale's *Pio Nono* (New York: P.J. Kennedy, 1954).

15. See Benedetto Croce, *History of the Kingdom of Naples* (Chicago: Chicago University Press, 1925), and Harold Acton, *The Last Bourbons of Naples* (London: Methuen, 1957).

16. G.F.H. and J. Berkeley's trilogy *Italy in the Making* (Cambridge: Cambridge University Press, 1932), is a valuable piece of consensus history.

17. Though Luigi Salvatorelli's *Pensiero e Azione del Risorgimento* (Torino: Einaudi, 1960) is considered the best work on Cavour and the *Risorgimento,* Dennis Mack Smith's *Cavour and Garibaldi, 1860: A Study in Political Conflict* (Cambridge: Cambridge University Press 1954) is also highly regarded.

18. Christopher Hibbert's *Garibaldi and His Enemies* (Boston: Little Brown, 1965), is a well-written relatively recent work on this popular subject.

19. See Shephard Bancroft Clough and Salvatore Saladino, *A History of Modern Italy* (New York: Columbia University Press, 1968), *passim.*

20. The major histories of the House of Savoy are only available in French and Italian. S. Guichenon's 3 volume *Histoire de la maison di Savoie* was published from 1777 to 1780. It contains valuable information about the family's history from 1056 to Victor Amadeus II, the first King of Sardinia. L. Cibrario's two volume *Origine e progressi della monarchia di Savoia* (1869) is particularly valuable for its description of the *Risorgimento.* A more recent,

but impressionistic work, is N. Brancaccio's *Dal nido Savoiardo al Trono d'Italia* (1930). Robert Katz's *The Fall of the House of Savoy* (New York: Macmillan, 1971), is a vulgar attempt available in English.

21. See Federico Chabod's *Storia della politica estera dal 1870-1896* (Bari: G. Laterza, 1965), for an analysis of the policies of the *Destra Storica* and *Sinistra Storica*.

22. See John W. Briggs, *An Italian Passage* (New Haven: Yale University Press, 1978), pp. 15-64, for a detailed description of the role of these mutual aid societies in the life of southern Italians.

23. See Federico Chabod, *Storia della politica estera Italiana dal 1870-1896*.

24. See Andrew Rolle, *The Immigrant Upraised* (Norman, Oklahoma: University of Oklahoma Press, 1974), pp. 42-76, *passim*.

25. See *Atti della Giunta parlamentare per la Inchiesta agraria e sulle condizioni della classe agricola,* 1883-1886, (15 volumes). This work contains data concerning losses in the region. It is generally critical of contemporary work habits, but does admit that taxes were unfairly proportioned.

26. See Christopher Seton-Watson, *Italy from Liberalism to Fascism, 1870-1925* (London: Oxford University Press, 1967), for a recent scholarly perspective on Crispi's administration. Benedetto Croce's *A History of Italy, 1871-1915* (London: Oxford University Press, 1929), is an impressionistic insider's view of the workings of the Italian government during this period. This work is particularly valuable because it is written by one of the great intellectuals of the twentieth century, who happened to be a Neapolitan.

27. See Roberto Tremelloni, *Storia dell'industria Italiana contemporanea,* 1947, for a study of Italy's emergence into the industrial era.

28. See *chapter 5* below for a description of George Scigliano.

29. *Boston Traveler,* May 31, 1904.

30. Much is written on the Giolitti Era. William Salamone's *Italian Democracy in the Making, 1900-1914: The Giolittian Era* (Philadelphia: University of Pennsylvania Press, 1945), is still the best work available in English.

31. See Pier Carlo Masini, *Storia degli anarchici italiani da Bakunin a Malatesta* (Turin: Rizzoli, 1973), for a valuable analysis of the anarchistic movement in Italy. More work is necessary on the topics of Italian socialism and Italian anarchism in the United States.

32. See Count Carlo Sforza, *Contemporary Italy,* (1944), and Benedetto Croce, *Storia d'Italia, 1871-1915,* (1929), for opposing views on the merits of the Giolitti reforms. The former finds it necessary to deprecate Giolitti in order to show a need for the reforms of Benito Mussolini. The latter, on the other hand, is generally complimentary of Giolitti's policies which he partially helped to formulate.

33. See "Avellino," *Enciclopedia Italiana,* (Roma: Istituto della Enciclopedia Italiana, 1934), v. 5, pp. 612-14, for a description of the Province of Avellino.

Chapter 2

1. As cited in Paula Todisco, *Boston's First Neighborhood: The North End* (Boston Public Library, 1976), p. 20. See Oscar Handlin, *Boston's Immigrants* (Cambridge: Harvard University Press, 1941), *passim,* for a comprehensive treatement of the Irish settlement in the North End.

2. See Walter Firey, *Land Use in Central Boston* (Cambridge: Harvard University Press, 1947), p. 171.

3. The reasons for this mistrust are described in chapter 1.

4. This information is taken from the oral statements of lifelong residents of the community. See the appendix for a complete list of those interviewed.

5. Taken from August 4, 1977, interview of Anthony Poto.

6. The "Padrone System" was a contract labor system. For a description of its use in Boston see chapter 5.

7. For a detailed analysis of the dimensions of Italian repatriation and seasonal employment in the United States, see Betty Boyd Caroli, *Italian Repatriation from the United States 1900-1914* (New York: Center for Migration Studies, 1973).

8. Several such works are Francesco Leveroni *Venticinque Anni di Missione fra gli Italiani Immigrati di Boston, Mass.* (Milano: Tipografia Santa Legia Eucaristica, 1913), and the popular weekly newspaper *La Gazetta del Massachusetts,* James V. Donnaruma, editor (Boston), 1903-1930. Leveroni, for example, wrote (p. 58) that there were 8,000 Italians in Boston in 1880, which is a figure four times higher than most other sources.

9. Most Italian immigrants remained in the North End, but some, usually because of employment reasons or in search of a small tract of land for a vegetable garden, moved to neighboring areas of the city, such as Charlestown, the West End, and East Boston.

10. See Robert Woods, *Americans in Process* (Boston: Houghton Mifflin, 1903), p. 42.

11. See Francesco Leveroni, *Venticinque Anni di Missione,* p. 58. The Italian text reads: "Essi erano Genovesi in massima parte. I meridionali, specialmente i Siciliani, constituivano la minoranza."

12. A. Frangini, *Italiani in Boston, Massachusetts* (Boston: Stamperia Commerciale, 1907), pp. 21-25, 53-54.

13. See Frederick Bushee, "Italian Immigrants in Boston" *The Arena* 17 (April, 1897), pp. 722-34.

14. Robert A. Woods, *Americans in Process,* p. 43.

15. See A. Frangini, *Italiani in Boston, Massachusetts, passim,* and William Foote Whyte, "Race Conflicts in the North End," *New England Quarterly* 21 (December, 1939), pp. 630-40.

16. Irving Howe's *World of Our Fathers—The Journey of the East European Jews to America and the Life They Found and Made* (New York: Simon and Schuster, 1976), is the most significant modern work concerning the topic. Though it is concerned with New York City, the first two chapters contain valuable material concerning living conditions and causes of Jewish emigration from Eastern Europe during the period under consideration here. Robert Weider's *The Early Jewish Community of Boston's North End* (Waltham, Massachusetts: Brandeis University Press, 1962), is a brief but commendable sociological study concerning the Russian and Polish Jewish history in Boston's North End from 1870 to 1900. My comments concerning the North End Jewish community are partially based on an interview with Samuel Gurwitz, a North End resident of the period, October 30, 1979.

17. So significant was the transformation from Yankee, Nova Scotian, and Celtic stock to Italians and Eastern European Jews during the last twenty years of the nineteenth century

that Samuel Adams Drake, a Yankee journalist and member of the Immigration Restriction League of Boston, felt compelled to revise a section of his popular 1872 work. While Drake had originally written commendably about the neighborhood, in 1906 he told a different story:

> No where in Boston has father time wrought such ruthless changes, as in the once highly respectable quarter, now swarming with Italians in every dirty nook and corner. In truth, it is hard to believe the evidence of our senses, though the fumes of garlic are sufficiently convincing. Past and present confront each other here with a stare of blank amazement, in the humble Revere homestead, on one side, and the pretentious Hotel Italy on the other; nor do those among us, who recall something of its vanished prestige, feel at all at home in a place where our own mother-tongue no longer serves us.

18. See Sam Bass Warner's *Streetcar Suburbs: The Process of Growth in Boston 1870-1900* (New York: Atheneum, 1969), p. 35. This is a classic study concerning the development of "the suburb" in American society. See also, Stephan Thernstrom's *The Other Bostonians: Poverty and Progress in the American Metropolis, 1880-1970* (Cambridge: Harvard University Press, 1973), p. 213.

19. Estimates concerning the location of Italian subcultural enclaves have been made based on information found in seven sources: (1) A. Frangini, *Italiani in Boston, Massachusetts* (Boston: Stamperia Commerciale, 1907); (2) Francesco Leveroni, *Venticinque Anni di Missione fra gl'Immigrati Italiani di Boston, Mass., 1888-1913* (Milano: Tipografia Santa Lega Eucaristica, 1913); (3) Robert A. Woods, *Americans In Process* (Boston: Houghton Mifflin, 1903); (4) *Boston City Directories,* 1899, 1909, 1919, 1929; (5) *La Gazzetta del Massachusetts* (Boston, 1903-1930); (6) Sacramental Records, Sacred Heart Italian Church and Saint Leonard of Port Maurice Church, Boston; (7) Oral history taken from individuals whose North End experiences dated back to 1890. No one of these sources was used as the main reference. Rather, all of them combined reflected a composite image of the neighborhood upon which I based my conclusions. Further, it must be stated that at no time do I infer that *only* one particular subculture lived in a particular block of tenements. What I do maintain, however, is that enclaves designated as the habitat of a particular group were *predominantly* occupied by the group in question.

20. For a description of "Avellino," see *Enciclopedia Italiano* (Roma: Istituto della Enciclopedia Italiano, 1934), vol. 5, pp. 612-14.

21. See Robert F. Foerster, *Italian Emigration of Our Times* (New York: Arno, 1919), *passim,* for a detailed description of Italian emigration to South America. Marco Caliaro and Marco Francesconi, *L'Apostolo degli Emigranti: Giovanni Battista Scalabrini, Vescovo di Piacenza* (Milano: Editrice Ancora, 1968), *passim,* provides a detailed account of the role the Catholic Church played in Italian emigration to South America.

Chapter 3

1. See *United States Senate Report of the Immigration Commission* (Washington: Government Printing Office, 1910), vols. 26-27.

2. Since its publication, the Dillingham Commission Report has received much criticism, most notably from Isaac A. Hourwich, *Immigration and Labor: The Economic Aspects of European Immigration to the United States* (New York), as early as 1912, and more recently from Oscar Handlin, *Race and Nationality in American Life* (Boston: Little Brown) in 1957.

Professor Handlin's work provides both original material and an historiography of the previous half century concerning the Dillingham Report. The major criticism has centered around the restrictionist bias of the commission, and its interpretation of the data, while the statistical materials presented have generally been accepted as accurate.

3. See chapter 1.

4. For example, C. Pappas, a well known Greek entrepreneur and founder of Pappas Importers, Incorporated, owned the Gloria Grocery Store at the corner of Richmond and North Streets at the beginning of the twentieth century. The report, however, said that the North End was second to Broadway in South Boston in number of Greek households (vol. 26, p. 434). As was the case so often here, general conclusions tended to be misleading. This may have been a popular neighborhood for Greeks, but they certainly must have constituted a distinct minority. By the report's own statistics (vol. 27, p. 21), of the 474 households sampled in the two North End "districts," only 10, or 2.1 percent were Greek.

Oral testimony showed that there was a Norwegian grocery merchant on Prince Street. The existence of three Norwegian and four Swedish heads of household may have been attributable to the North End proximity to the fishing and merchant fleets. They may have been longtime residents of the area. Since no information beyond their existence was offered, any hypothesis could be valid. No other source used by this author, described the existence of Swedes or Norwegians in the North End.

5. *United States Senate Report of the Immigration Commission, v. 26, pp. 430-36.*

6. The high number of non-Jewish Poles and Lithuanians seemed strange at first because none of the church records at Sacred Heart, Saint Leonard, or Saint Mary show any Polish or Lithuanian members. Saint Stephen's Church records do show the existence of a small Polish congregation of about 200 members, but this was for only two and one-half years (1916-1919). The identification of where the non-Jewish Poles and Lithuanians worshipped was important because it would have verified the findings of the report as well as the validity of the church records. It is safe to assume that these Poles and Lithuanians were Catholics. The devout nature of Polish and Lithuanian Catholics ruled out the possibility of their summary rejection of traditional Catholic practices. One interviewee, who asked to remain anonymous, identified the existence of a Polish "social club" on Chambers Street in the West End while reminiscing about her teenage years. "My sister and I, along with some girlfriends, went to the Polish Club once or twice for a dance. Our parents would not have been too pleased, but we thought it was all right because the club was part of a church." A check of the Catholic Chancery Office records revealed that on September 13, 1920, the Polish Church of Our Lady of Ostrabrama was dedicated next to a small Polish "social club" on Chambers Street. This church was built by the North End Polish community, which had previously occupied the basement of Saint Stephen's Church in the North End—a practice the Irish Catholics forced upon Italians who were required to use a storefront church rather than Saint Mary's main sanctuary.

The existence of the Lithuanian community proved to be more difficult to verify. No English language material was discovered in our attempt. Even the Catholic Chancery Office was of no assistance. Father William Wolkovich, a scholar of Lithuanian studies, suggested the possibility that they may have worshipped at either Saint Rocco's in Brockton, Saint Peter's in South Boston, or Immaculate Conception in East Cambridge. Since only Immaculate Conception was within walking distance of the North End, it seemed the most likely choice. Its sacramental records clearly show that this was the church of the North End Lithuanian community from 1910, when it was first acquired.

7. The *United States Senate Report of the Immigration Commission,* 1910, v. 26, p. 437.

8. *The United States Senate Report of the Immigration Commission,* 1910, v. 26, p. 436.

9. Julius Drachsler's *Intermarriage in New York City* (New York: Columbia University Press), 1921, is the classic study of immigrant intermarriage and intramarriage in New York. Using Sacramental Records, Drachsler shows (p. 173) that 96.9 percent of all New York Italians married other Italians from 1908 to 1912. Northern Italians married other northern Italians at a 81.8 percent rate (p. 174), and southern Italians at a 15.6 percent rate. Southern Italians married other southern Italians at a 90.7 percent rate, and northern Italians at a 4.2 percent rate (p. 122). A more recent study of 1960 intramarriage among first generation Italians is Hugh Carter and Paul Glick's *Marriage and Divorce: A Social and Economic Study* (Cambridge: Harvard University Press), 1970. The authors conclude that even in the 1960s, Italians married other Italians at a 64 percent rate (p. 133), which was the highest among the eight groups sampled. In 1978, John W. Briggs, *An Italian Passage,* (New Haven: Yale University Press), analyzed the Italian immigrant intramarriage rate by provinces, from 1912 to 1915, in Utica and Rochester, New York. He concluded that more than 90 percent of all Italians sampled married other Italians. Though he attempts to identify Italian provincial intermarriage and intramarriage, no consistent pattern is identified city to city, other than the fact that women had a slightly higher intramarriage rate than men.

10. See chapter 4 for a history of the founding of these churches.

11. Dr. Silvano Tomasi, the Editor of *International Migration Review,* stated that a sample of 3 percent to 5 percent was acceptable for a study of this sort. Professor Rudolph Vecoli, Director of the Immigration History Research Center, University of Minnesota, concurred, adding that an 8 percent sample should reflect a very accurate profile.

12. Tillie Sablone (see photo) was born on Hanover Street, Boston, in 1905, of Abruzzesi parents. She married Vincenzo Sablone (see photo) in 1928. Vincenzo, later Americanized and known as James, was born in Pescara, Abruzzi, near Tillie's town of ancestry.

13. The 26 provinces mentioned were: in *Sicily*-Agrigento, Caltanisetta, Girgenti, Messina, Palermo, Siracusa, Trapani, Catania; in *Calabria*-Reggio di Calabria, Catanzaro, Cosenza; in *Basilicata*-Matera, Potenza; in *Puglie*-Ariano, Bari, Brindisi, Lecce, Taranto; in *Abruzzi*-Campobasso, Pescara, L'Aquila; in *Campania*-Avellino, Benevento, Caserta, Napoli, Salerno.

14. See chapter 1 for an explanation of *stranieri.*

15. Gaetano Grande (see photo) migrated to Boston in 1906. He owned a barber shop in North Square until his death in 1972. His shop, which is now operated by his sons Paul and Domenic, has always been identified as a "Neapolitan shop." Domenic said that "the Sicilian shop" before World War I was on the first floor of the historic Moses Pierce Hitchborn House (Paul Revere's father-in-law) adjacent to Paul Revere's House in North Square.

Chapter 4

1. See Silvano M. Tomasi, "The Ethnic Church and the Integration of Italian Immigrants in the United States," *The Italian Experience in the United States* (New York: Center for Migration Studies, 1970), *passim,* and *Piety and Power: The Role of Italian Parishes in the New York Metropolitan Area* (New York: Center for Migration Studies, 1975), *passim.*

2. See Rudolph J. Vecoli, "Prelates and Peasants: Italian Immigrants and the Catholic Church" *Journal of Social History* 2 (Spring, 1969), pp. 217-67.

3. An examination of the *Catholic Directory* (New York: Sadlier and Company), 1868-1900, shows a preponderance of Irish names listed among the clergy of Boston. In only one section of volume three of Robert Lord, *et al., History of the Catholic Archdiocese of Boston* (New York: Sheed and Ward, 1944) is the Irish influence not stressed. That section is entitled "Newer Catholic Races."

4. There was an active Protestant missionary effort among the Italians of Boston at the turn of the century. The North End had Italian Baptist, Methodist, Episcopalian, and Congregational churches during this period. For more information concerning Protestant missionary work among North End Italians, see Francis DeBilio, *Protestant Mission Work Among Italians in Boston* (Ph.D. Dissertation, Boston University, 1949).

5. *Lumen Gentium* ("The Constitution on the Church in the Modern World"), 1965, was the major document issued at the conclusion of the Second Vatican Council of the Roman Catholic Church. It gave national councils of bishops the responsibility of developing greater lay input at the parochial level. In the United States parish councils have been formed, but they are still mostly advisory, with the pastor retaining the right to overrule any decision of the parish council.

6. See chapter 1 for a description of the unification of Italy, and its social impact on the peasant classes.

7. Nicholas J. Russo, *The Religious Acculturation of the Italians in New York City* (Ph.D. Dissertation, St. John's University, 1968) studies the church attendance practices of Italian-Americans in New York into the second generation. Though a national pattern is not established, this study attempts to show that Italian males at least in New York City continued to be less regular churchgoers than the female even after two generations.

   Harold Abramson's *Ethnic Diversity in Catholic America,* (New York: John Wiley, 1973), is also of value because it discusses persistent Italian male religious values into the third generation in America.

8. See chapter 1 above for a description of *campanilismo.*

9. Italian-Americans to this day balk at having to pay what one person interviewed called "an entrance fee" for church attendance. Several Italians interviewed pointed out that Church Law specifically forbids this "Irish practice."

10. See "Memoranda of the Diocese of Boston" April 15, 1866, Archives of the Catholic Archdiocese of Boston (henceforth referred to as ACAB).

11. See Leonard Bacigalupo, *The Franciscans and Italian Immigration in America* (Wappingers Falls, New York: Mount Alvernia Friary, 1973).

12. The Diocese of Boston was raised to the rank of an archdiocese on February 12, 1875. Bishop John Williams was subsequently titled an archbishop.

13. See *The Pilot,* June 7, 1869.

14. See *Early Parish File,* Saint Mary's Church, ACAB, for a description of the controversy which preceded the transfer of the church to the Society of Jesus.

15. Marco Caliaro and Mario Francesconi, *John Baptist Scalabrini: Apostle to Emigrants* (New York: Center for Migration Studies, 1977), and Coleman Barry, *The Catholic Church and German Americans* (Milwaukee: Bruce, 1953) mention some of the structures first used for religious services by Italian and German immigrants respectively.

16. The ACAB contain the only copy of an unpublished and undated biography of Archbishop John Williams, written by Mother Augustine of Carmel. Mother Augustine was a childhood neighbor of John Williams in their youth. Consequently, there are many valuable personal reminiscences here. This lengthy biography (more than 800 typed pages), however, suffers from a lack of scholarship. Cardinal O'Connell, who commissioned the work, refused to publish it for this reason. There are several letters in the file which would indicate that the biography was written about 1920. Cardinal O'Connell's refusal may have also been partly due to his "unsympathetic" impression of his predecessor, who Mother Augustine portrays as a saintly prelate.

17. This was the site of the Samuel Mather Church in colonial Boston. See Annie Thwing, *Crooked and Narrow Streets of Boston* (Boston: Marshall Jones, 1920), p. 53.

18. See *Early Parishes File,* Saint John the Baptist Church, Boston, ACAB.

19. Father Emiliano Gerbi served the Italian community at St. Mary's Church, Charlestown, from 1862 to 1866. From 1866 to 1868 he was assigned to the Cathedral of the Holy Cross in the South End of Boston. He was subsequently appointed pastor of Gate of Heaven Parish in that same community. He died in 1873.

20. For information concerning early Franciscan work in Boston see John LoConte, *The Catholic Church and the Italian Immigrant Colony of Boston,* (M.A. thesis, Washington: Catholic University, 1968), *passim,* and Leonard Bacigalupo, "The Franciscans and Italian Immigration in America," *The Religious Experience of Italian Americans* (American Italian Historical Association Proceedings, 6th Annual Conference, November, 1973), pp. 107-121.

21. Father Gerbi was held in such esteem by the mostly Irish congregation at Gate of Heaven Church in the South End of Boston that, upon his death, the parishoners arranged that he be buried in Saint Augustine's Burial Ground. This burial site in South Boston is very special for the Catholic community of Boston and is the place of internment of the earliest bishops and twenty pioneer priests of the diocese.

22. See James Sullivan, *The Catholic Church in New England* (Boston: Holy Cross Press, 1895), p. 136. The ACAB do not contain any figures.

23. See the Episcopal Register, Bishop John Williams, 1873, ACAB.

24. John LoConte, *Italian Immigrant Colony of Boston* (1968) pp. 46-50 contains some interesting information concerning Father Guerrini's life during and after his assignment in Boston.

25. See *Old Parishes File,* Saint Leonard of Port Maurice Church, Boston, ACAB.

26. See Sullivan, *Catholic Church in New England,* p. 134.

27. See chapter 2 for North End population statistics.

28. Official Record of the Custody of the Immaculate Conception of the Friars Minor of Buffalo, New York, p. 24.

29. See the letter of Father Boniface to Father Leo, October 21, 1878, and the letter of Father Leo to Father Boniface, October 23, 1878, in the records of the Order of Friars Minor, Mount Alvernia Friary, Wappingers Falls, New York.

30. Father Joachim Guerrini was sent back to Italy in December, 1878. He left the Franciscan Order the following year, and subsequently went to Australia as a missionary priest. From

1880 until his death in 1918, he became one of the most noted missionaries in New South Wales, Australia.

31. See the letter of Father Leo to Archbishop Williams, November 20, 1878, ACAB.

32. See chapter 3 for a detailed description of the North Italian regions represented in the North End population at this time.

33. The earliest North End Italians were from Genoa. All northern Italians were subsequently referred to as "Genoese" by the local Italian population.

34. See "Diary of the *Societa' San Marco,*" Archives of the Center for Migration Studies, Staten Island, New York.

35. This was near the site of the original Old North Church. See the M.A. thesis of William DeMarco *Topography of the North End of Boston on the Eve of the American Revolution* (Bridgewater State College, 1976), pp. 30-34.

36. May 17, 1884, an article appeared in the *Boston Herald* which described "Father Boniface Bragantini's Troubles with His Italian Flock." This article described the impasse from the view of the Genoese community. The following day, Father Boniface, upset with the *Boston Herald* management for the article, wrote a letter to the rival *Boston Globe* in which he stated that he was the pastor of all Italians in the community, and could not cater to one particular faction. As a result of this confrontation, Father Boniface did not get any Genoese financial support, which was essential for success of "his plan" to purchase the Bethel.

37. Giovanni Battista Scalabrini (1839-1905), was ordained a priest in 1863, and consecrated Bishop of Piacenza, a city in northern Italy, in 1876. He frequently spoke out against the failures of Italy's emigration policy. In 1887, he founded the *Associazione di Patronato per l'Emigrazione,* based on the model of the German Saint Raphael Soceity—an immigrant aid group. That same year, he formed the Missionary Society of Saint Charles, for the care of Italian emigrants worldwide. Bishop Scalabrini sent Father Francis Zaboglio (see photo) from Italy to resolve the San Marco Society impasse, and to serve the congregation at the new church in North Square. During the summer of 1901, Bishop Scalabrini met with President Theodore Roosevelt at the White House to discuss American care for Italian immigrants. During that visit to the United States, he visited the North Square congregation. While there are a dozen works available in Italian on the life of John Scalabrini, there are only two biographies in English. Both works are translations of Italian texts. They are *Father to the Immigrants* by Icilio Felici (New York: P.J. Kennedy, 1955); and *John Baptist Scalabrini: Apostle to Emigrants* by Marco Caliaro and Mario Francesconi (New York: Center for Migration Studies, 1977).

38. See "Archbishop Williams-San Marco Society File," ACAB, letters from Cardinal Simeoni to Archbishop Williams dated June 7, 1866, August 31, 1886, and April 1887. In these letters Cardinal Simeoni states how he encouraged the *Societa' San Marco* to relinquish its demand to maintain ownership of the church property in favor of the archbishop. Their continued insistence that the "Franciscans must go" reflected just how deep was their conviction that the Franciscan Friars were not terribly concerned about the welfare of these Genoese immigrants.

39. The society paid $28,000 for the Bethel: $10,000 cash, and $18,000 mortgaged. The *Societa' San Marco* managed to raise $10,000 within a one-month period. For further details see Francesco Leveroni, et al. *Venticinque anni di Missione fra gli Italiani Immigrati di Boston, Massachusetts* (Milano: Tipografica Santa Lega Eucaristica, 1913), p. 58.

40.   The "problem" of the recent Catholic immigrant was one of the major reasons the Third
      Plenary Council of Baltimore was convened in the Fall of 1884. Archbishop Williams's
      negative response to the request of the *Societa' San Marco* no doubt reflected some of the
      attitudes developed in Baltimore. At that council, Archbishop Williams was a member of
      the "Committee on Italian Colonies" (*De Colonis Italianis*), and chairman of the
      "Committee on New Business" (*De Re Nova*). The former committee was specifically
      formed at the request of Cardinal Simeoni, the Prefect of the Congregation for the
      Propagation of the Faith in Rome. As such, he was the superior of all bishops throughout
      the world, and accountable directly to the pope for their actions. Archbishop Williams,
      along with Corrigan of New York, McQuaid of Rochester, Spaulding of Peoria, and de
      Goesbriand of Burlington (Vermont), decided that, since they could only speak disparaging-
      ly of the Italians, the committee should say something positive about work American
      bishops were doing with other immigrant groups. They then proceeded to write a glowing
      account of the charitable works of the Irish Immigration Society. Bishop McQuaid was
      given the task of informing Pope Leo XIII of the results of their work. In a June 17, 1885,
      letter to Archbishop Gibbons of Baltimore, McQuaid said: "My letter to the pope shall be
      carefully worded, yet quite as firmly as usual. It is a very delicate matter to tell the sovereign
      pontiff how utterly faithless the specimens of his country coming here really are. Ignorance
      of their religion and a depth of vice little known to us yet, are their prominent
      characteristics." They specifically addressed the issue of German Catholic practices in Saint
      Louis and Minneapolis, where there seemed to be major discontent.

      The activities of Archbishop Williams at the Third Plenary Council of Baltimore were
      barely a memory when he was approached by the *Societa' San Marco*. The importance of
      the Baltimore Council to the North End Italian community is underscored by the fact that
      the "Archbishop Williams-San Marco Society File," ACAB, contains several letters of
      Archbishop Williams to other bishops concerning the work at the council, as well as extracts
      from the council proceedings.

      For more information concerning the Italian tract see *"De zelo animarum, Caput I, De
      colonis et advenis,"* Acta et decreta concilii plenarii Baltimorensis tertii (Baltimore, 1884)
      pp. 76-77. See also *The Letterbook of James Gibbons,* Baltimore Cathedral Archives, 1884-
      1885, and Frederick J. Zwierlein, *The Life and Letters of Bishop McQuaid* (Rochester,
      1926), vol. 2, p. 335. Rev. Henry Browne's "The 'Italian Problem' in the Catholic Church of
      the United States," *U.S. Catholic Historical Society, Historical Records and Studies,*
      XXXV, 1946, pp. 46-72, is critical of the attitudes and policies of Archbishop Michael
      Corrigan of New York and Bishop Bernard McQuaid of Rochester towards Italian
      immigrants. The author points out their less than objective statements at the Third Plenary
      Council of Baltimore, their opposition to the creation of national parishes, and their
      subsequent indirect reprimand by Pope Leo XIII.

      Philip Gleason and David Salvaterra, "Ethnicity Immigration and American Catholic
      History," *Social Thought,* 4 (Summer, 1978), pp. 3-28, is a more recent work on nineteenth-
      century problems concerning the administration of national parishes. The conclusions
      drawn here differ from those of Henry Browne. Gleason and Salvaterra believe that the
      American Catholic hierarcy was less at fault than the local pastors of territorial parishes,
      who feared a loss of a portion of their congregation, and their subsequent support.

41.   See Francesco Gregori, *La Vita e L'Opera di un grande Vescovo* (Torino, 1934), p. 412.

42.   Joseph Tassinari, a Genoese by birth, is a septuagenarian. He has been a member of Sacred
      Heart Church his entire life, and a member of the Saint Mark Society since 1934. Both his

father and uncle were among the founding members of the *Societa' San Marco*. The earliest records of the *Societa' San Marco* were given by Joseph Tassinari to the Center for Migration Studies, Staten Island, New York, in 1976.

43. See chapter 3 above, "New World Enclave-Old World Marriage," for an analysis of the marriage records of both churches.

44. See chapter 1 for a description of *campanalismo,* and its importance in Italian life.

45. Taken from the December 13, 1976, interview of Pat Voto, who is also mentioned in chapter 5 below.

46. Taken from September, 1979, interview of William De Marco, Sr., the father of the author. (See photo).

47. Alfredo Tassinari died in 1978. He migrated to the United States in 1879, living more than ninety-nine years in Boston. He still spoke with an accent, reflecting the very strong influence of his Italian upbringing. He became a member of the *Societa' San Marco* in 1894, joining his father and uncle. His sense of humor and remarkably vivid memory remained with him until his death.

48. Leveroni's *Venticinque Anni di Missione . . .* (1913) is of particular value here, as is the *Gazzetta del Massachusetts,* which frequently recorded the activities of the religious societies in the North End.

49. See the appendix for a complete list of religious societies.

50. See Leveroni, *Venticinque Anni di Missione . . .,* (1913), pp. 41-54.

51. There is a distinct possibility that these two groups may have belonged to the Italian Episcopalian Church of Saint Francis of Assissi on Salem Street. Many Northern Italians left the Catholic Church as a result of the San Marco Society incident mentioned above, and found a more welcome reception waiting for them in the neighborhood's newly formed Italian protestant churches. For more information concerning Protestant work among North End Italians, see Francis DeBilio, *Protestant Mission Work among Italians in Boston* (Ph.D. Dissertation, Boston University, 1949).

52. See Anna Martellone, *Una Little Italy nell'Atene d'America* (Napoli: Guida Editori, 1973), pp. 577-80.

Chapter 5

1. In 1945, Carl Wittke, an immigration scholar particularly known for his work concerning German migration to the United States, wrote the respected general work *We Who Built America* (New York: Prentice Hall). In a chapter entitled "The Italians," he described the Italian work experience in a manner representative of the genre:

   > Before 1860, Italian migration consisted largely of vendors of plaster statuary, organ grinders with their monkeys, and political refugees. . . . Later in the nineteenth century the newcomers were transplanted from their sunny Italian hill farms to the railroad and mining camps and to the construction gangs of American cities. . . . Hard work, low wages, large families, tenement houses, poor food, and saloons tell the story of the maladjustment of the first and second generations. Crimes of violence rank particularly high among them. [p. 438]

   Stephan Thernstrom, in his *The Other Bostonians* (Cambridge: Harvard University Press, 1973), described the "slow upward mobility" (p. 253) of Boston's Italians, *vis à vis* the

Yankees, Irish, Jews and Blacks. He stated that the stereotype did not fit, because both Italians and Jews experienced similar initial employment handicaps—poor initial financial status, inadequate English language skills, lack of formal education (pp. 166, 208, 232), and yet the Jews achieved a far greater level of upward economic mobility in the first and second generations. His study, however, failed to analyze the importance of Italian enclaves in the employment process. He erroneously dismissed the need for such research when he stated: "Ethnic groups were too transient to allow for a study of their persistence in *any* (italics mine) Boston neighborhood. There were indeed Irish, Italian, Jewish, and other ethnic neighborhoods that could easily be discerned, but the vast majority of anonymous immigrants who lived in them at one census were destined to vanish from them before 10 years had elapsed" (p. 232). My research shows that North End Italians were certainly not so transient, and that upward economic mobility was not necessarily tied to any out-migration. For an evaluation of the methodology used by Thernstrom, see Richard S. Alcorn and Peter R. Knights, "Most Uncommon Bostonians: A Critique of Stephan Thernstrom's *The Other Bostonians, 1880-1970," Historical Methods Newsletter* 8, no. 3 (June, 1975), pp. 98-114.

2. See the Appendix for a list of the companies which employed North End Italians in 1909, as identified by the *Boston City Directory.*

3. See chapter 1 for a description of the role of the father in an Italian family.

4. A recent series of requests of the City of Boston Records Division elicited the following statement from one of the director's there: "There are many mistakes with Italian records from before 1930."

5. Volumes 26 and 27 analyzed Italian work patterns in seven American cities, including Boston. Oscar Handlin, in his *Race And Nationality in American Life* (Boston: Little Brown and Company, 1957) analyzes the entire Dillingham Commission Report's methodology and conclusions. He found the report to be neither scientific nor impartial. He found fault with three procedures in particular. First, the commission did not hold public hearings. Second, no witness was ever cross-examined by commission members—the statements of the experts who compiled the data were always accepted at face value. Third, the final report was adopted within a half hour of the time when, under law, it had to be filed. The commission's failure to make use of any occupation data other than that which was accumulated by its own staff contributed to the report's inadequacies.

6. James Sablone (see photo) migrated to the North End in 1909. He volunteered to return to Italy to fight to protect the "paese," along with his four brothers. He was the only one of the five to return to the United States. He retired in the early 1960s, and died in 1978.

7. Joseph Cassia (see photo) migrated to the United States in 1912, from Siracusa, Sicily. He volunteered to return to Italy to protect "the paese" during World War I. He lost his hearing in combat, and has been totally deaf since his engagement at the Brenner Pass. He presently lives in retirement in Revere, Massachusetts.

8. Joseph Tassinari is the president of the "San Marco Society." His family has resided in the North End since the 1880s.

9. Louis Reppucci was a retired contractor living in Medford, Massachusetts, at the time of this interview. His family migrated to the North End at the turn of the century.

10. See *Gazzetta del Massachusetts,* February 18, 1905, p. 1. The entire collection of the *Gazzetta,* which has been continuously published since 1903 by James and Caesar Donnaruma can be found in the "James V. Donnaruma Collection," Immigration History Research Center, University of Minnesota.

11. Paul Grande, though of retirement age, does not plan to stop barbering in the near future. He lives in an adjoining family-owned apartment building. He said his father continued to cut hair "on and off" until he was in his eighties.

12. Pasquale Verro is a retired restaurateur. He gave up the barber shop and trade late in the 1940s, and went into the more lucrative restaurant business. His family was from Calabria. He presently lives in retirement in Chelsea, Massachusetts.

13. One North End Genoese peddler who achieved uncommon wealth due to successful stock investments was John Deferrari, who lived well into his nineties. When he died in the mid-nineteen sixties he left the Boston Public Library a bequest of several million dollars for the construction of an addition to its main branch. The "Deferrari Room" is named after him.

14. The "Pastene Corporation," a major food importer now based in New York, first opened its doors as a Genoese grocery store at 229 Hanover Street in 1874. The "Genoa Packing Company," a large New England food processor, originally opened as a Genoese grocery store on North Street in the 1890s.

15. A. Frangini *Italiani in Boston, Mass.* (Boston: Stamperia Commerciale, 1907), pp. 21-25, 31, 41, 42, verifies the existence of these stores as early as 1871.

16. John Plescia owned and operated the Prince Pastry Shop on Prince Street since 1927. His shop has been given many "Best of Boston" awards.

17. Michael DeMarco, an uncle of the author, was born in the North End in 1904. He was very active in all of his father's business activities, which began in 1893 and ended with the ownership of a large limousine service in 1949.

18. For a description of the seedy aspects of pre-Italian North End life, see Robert A. Woods, *Americans in Process* (Boston: Houghton Mifflin, 1903), *passim.*

19. The Immigration History Research Center of the University of Minnesota contains many files which reflect the ongoing feud on the topic. The "James V. Donnaruma Collection," contains entire folders which relate directly to North End Italian involvement in organized crime. Folders 5, 6, 7, 8, 9, cover criminal activity in the community from 1910 to 1947. Letters of correspondence between the accused/convicted criminal and Mr. Donnaruma, and his tireless effort to ensure equal justice for the Italian immigrant, are ever-present. Folder 38 contains Italian-language newspaper clippings from throughout the United States on the same topic. Folders 54 to 67 have copies of his own newspaper, *La Gazzetta del Massachusetts,* from 1903 to 1955. The "George Scigliano Collection," also at IHRS, University of Minnesota, sheds light on the involvement of both Neapolitan and Sicilian crime groups in the North End from 1898 to 1907.

Prostitution involving Italian women is a field which has only recently been explored by scholars. The most important contributions to this area of research in recent years have been made by Mary Gibson of Grinnell College. Her *Urban Prostitution in Italy, 1860 to 1915: an Experiment in Social Control* (1978), and "Prostitution and Feminism in Late Nineteenth-Century Italy," (Toronto: The Multicultural History Society of Ontario, 1978), are the major revisionist works on the topic. Much of her work is based on medical records from Turin and Rome, Italy, from 1890 to 1905. She also utilizes many of the official Italian government records of the period.

20. *Boston Post,* Sunday, March 6, 1904.

21. *Boston Traveler,* August 20, 1904.

22. *Boston Post,* June 18, 1906.

23. The most widely respected work on the *padrone* system is the doctoral dissertation "Italian Immigration and the Impact of the Padrone System" by Luciano John Iorizzo, (Syracuse University), 1966. Much of this work has been incorporated into *The Italian-Americans,* Luciano Iorizzo and Salvatore Mondello, (Boston: Twayne Publishers), 1971. Professor Iorizzo's thesis is that, in spite of the fact that some of the labor agents were unscrupulous and exploited many of the immigrants, they generally aided in the immigrants' adjustment process. If the governments in question had acted in a more responsible manner towards these newest settlers, the exploitation and abuse would never have had to be tolerated to begin with.

    Professor Robert Harney, of the Multicultural History Society of Ontario, has written a major new work on the topic: *The Padrone System and Sojourners in the Canadian North, 1885-1920* (Toronto: MHSO, 1978). In this work, Professor Harney describes the role Italian labor merchants played in peopling the Canadian North County.

24. The port of Boston was used until 1905 by the White Star Line, with weekly arrivals from Italy. Facilities at the Charlestown Navy Yard were used for immigration processing. The passenger lists, and related documents, are presently deposited in a warehouse building at that site. They have not yet been made available for scholarly study.

25. The activities of the Stabile Bank were the object of a Canadian Government investigation in 1904. The royal inquiry found fault with the policies of the Canadian Antonio Cordasco, who had hired Stabile in 1901 to help with the building of the Canadian railroad system. Banco Stabile, however, did not receive any criticism for its activities in the matter. This investigation did identify the Boston and Maine Railroad as the mechanism by which Boston Italians were readily transported both to Maine and Ontario, Canada. Robert Harney's *The Padrone System and Sojourners in the Canadian North, 1885-1920* (Toronto: Multicultural History Society of Ontario, 1978) is a recent study which analyzes the work of Stabile (pp. 24-59) and other *padroni* in Canada at the turn of the century.

26. See the *James V. Donnaruma Collection,* Folder 11 (Medical Care), Immigration History Research Center, University of Minnesota, for material concerning North End physicians during the period from 1905-1940.

27. Dr. Frank Leonardi practiced dentistry in the North End from 1919 to 1965. He was also a practicing attorney, and served three terms in the Massachusetts State Legislature. He was a member of the board of directors of the Hendricks Club, a powerful political machine with Irish, Jewish, and Italian members.

28. George Scigliano achieved prominence in Boston as an attorney and legislator before his untimely death in 1907. His personal papers are available in the "George Scigliano Collection," Immigration History Research Center, University of Minnesota. The material provides a rare view of one of the most interesting political ethnic lives in turn of the century Boston.

29. One of the more interesting examples of this profession was Benedict DeBelfis. A page one July 16, 1921, story in *The Italian News* said: "Benedict DeBellis Received B.A. from Harvard in 3 Years, Though Totally Blind—This Year He Receives Law Degree from Boston University after only One Year of Study."

30. There is widespread interest among scholars concerning the role of Italian women in the Italian-American experience. Some of the more important research projects now in progress

include: Professor Francesca Collecchia, Duquesne University (Pittsburgh) "Three Generations of Italian Mothers of Pittsburgh—An Oral History"; Professor Mary Gibson, Grinnell
College (Iowa) "Urban Prostitution in Italy, 1860 to 1915: An Experiment in Social
Control," and an ongoing project concerning the impact of modern Italian women's history
on Italian-American society: Assistant Professor Judith Jeffrey Howard, George Washington University, "The Woman Question in Italy, 1861-1880"; Professor Colleen Johnson,
University of California (San Francisco), an anthropological study concerning family
support systems for the elderly among Southern Italians; Corinne A. Krause, New York
Institute on Pluralism and Group Identity, "Women, Ethnicity, and Mental Health";
Professor Emiliana Noether, University of Connecticut, is concerned with the differences
between Sardinian and southern Italian women: The Center for Migration Studies, Staten
Island, New York, is the headquarters of the American Italian Historical Association, which
acts as a clearinghouse and research facility for much of this research.

Three of the more interesting recently completed studies in the field are Robert Harney,
Silvano Tomasi, Betty Boyd Caroli, *The Italian Immigrant Woman in North America*
(Toronto: The Multicultural History Society of Ontario, 1978); Judith E. Smith, *Italian
Mothers, American Daughters: Changes in Work and Family Roles* (Ph.D. Dissertation,
Brown University, 1979); Sharon Hartman Strom, *Italian American Women and Their
Daughters in Rhode Island* (Ph.D. Dissertation, University of Rhode Island, 1979).

31.   See the *James V. Donnaruma Collection,* Folder 11, (Medical Care), Immigration History
Research Center, University of Minnesota, for material concerning both physicians and
nurses in the North end during the period from 1905-1940.

32.   See *James V. Donnaruma Collection,* IHRC, University of Minnesota, Folders 53 and 54,
for a description of North End Italians in the performing arts.

Bibliography

Manuscripts and Collections

Anthony Capraro Collection. Immigration History Research Center, University of Minnesota.
Caesar Donnaruma Collection. Immigration History Research Center, University of Minnesota.
James V. Donnaruma Collection. Immigration History Research Center, University of Minnesota
Emiliano Grandinetti Collection. Immigration History Research Center, University of Minnesota.
George LaPiana Collection. Andover-Harvard Theological Library, Harvard University.
Rosa Levis Collection. Radcliffe College.
San Marco Society Diary. Center for Migration Studies, Staten Island, New York.
George Scigliano Collection. Immigration History Research Center, University of Minnesota.
Bartolomeo Vanzetti Collection. Immigration History Research Center, University of Minnesota.
Archbishop John Williams Papers. Chancery Archives, Archdiocese of Boston.
Archbishop Williams-San Marco Society File. Chancery Archives, Archdiocese of Boston.

Official Records

Abbott, Grace, *The Problem of Immigration in Massachusetts—Report of the Commission on Immigration.* Boston, 1914.
Baptist Bethel Log Book. Boston, 1893-1927.
Boston City Dirctory. 1880-1931.
Boston Police Department, Precinct One. Records, 1880-1927
Commissariato Generale dell'Emigrazione. *Annuario Statistico dell'Emigrazione Italiana,* Roma, 1926.
Commissariato Generale dell'Emigrazione. *Bolletino dell'Emigrazione.* Roma, 1902-1926.
Commissariato Generale dell'Emigrazione. *L'Emigrazione Italiana.* Roma, 1925.
Direzione Generale della Statistica. *Statistica della Emigrazione Italiana.* Roma, 1896-1914.
Istituto Centrale di Statistica. *Sommario di Statistiche Italiane: 1861-1955,* (Roma), 1958.
New England Conference Minutes. First Italian Methodist Church. Boston, 1895-1927.
_____. Saint Paul's Italian Methodist Church. Boston.
Old Parishes File. Chancery. Catholic Archdiocese of Boston.
Sacred Heart Church Parish Records. Boston, 1887-1927.
Saint Francis of Assissi Italian Episcopal Chapel Records. Boston, 1917-1927.
Saint John the Baptist Church Parish Records. Boston, 1884-1910.
Saint Leonard's Church Parish Records. Boston, 1878-1927.

Saint Mary's Church Parish Records. Boston, 1875-1927.

Saint Stephen's Church Parish Records. Boston, 1875-1927.

U.S. Bureau of the Census. *Statistical Abstract of the Thirteenth Census of the United States.* Washington, 1913.

U.S. Bureau of the Census. *Statistical Abstract of the Fourteenth Census of the United States.* Washington, 1923.

U.S. Commissioner General of Immigration. *Annual Report.* Washington, 1891-1920.

U.S. Congress. *Report on the Importation of Contract Labor.* 2 vol. Washington, 1889.

U.S. Immigration Commission, 1907-1910. *Reports of the Immigration Commission.* 42 vol. Washington, 1910.

Newspapers

Bolletino dell'emigrazione. Roma, 1898-1920.

Boston American. 1810-1927.

Boston Globe, 1880-1927.

Boston Herald, 1880-1927.

Boston Post, 1894-1911.

Boston Traveler, 1880-1927.

Gazzetta del Massachusetts, Boston, 1903-1927.

Il Progresso Italo-Americano. New York, 1890-1927.

Il Proletario. Boston, 1918.

Italica Gens. Torino, Italy, 1906-1918.

La Notizia. Boston, 1918.

La Tribuna del Popolo. Boston, 1915.

L'Emigrato Italiano. Piacenza, Italy, 1914-1920.

The Italian News. Boston, 1921-1927.

The Pilot. Boston, 1810-1930.

Maps

Barta Press. "Block Maps—Vicinity of Faneuil Hall, Boston," (*map 81.3.1897.2, Boston Public Library).

Fagan, James. "Shawmut—1630, Boston—1930," 1928 (map 984.24.B5, BPL).

"Map of Boston Proper," 1894 (*map 81.3, BPL).

"Outline Plan Showing Growth of Boston," 1880 (*map 81.3, BPL).

Winsor, Justin. "Boston Old and New," 1880 (BPL).

Dissertations and Master's Theses

Bauer, John. "Economic and Social Conditions of the Italians in the United States." Ph.D. dissertation, Yale University, 1908.

Bayer, Allen F. "The Assimilation of American Family Patterns by European Immigrants and Their Children." Ph.D dissertation, Florida State University, 1965.

Bere, Mary. "A Comparative Study of the Medical Capacity of Children of Foreign Parentage." Ph.D. dissertation, Columbia University, 1924.

Berger, Morris Isaiah. "The Settlement, The Immigrant, and The Public School." Ph.D. dissertation, Columbia University, 1956.

Berrol, Selma C. "Immigrants at School New York City, 1898-1914." Ph.D. dissertation, City University of New York, 1967.

Birnbaum, Lucia D. "Behaviorists, Protestants and Progressives 1913-1933." Ph.D. dissertation, University of California at Berkeley, 1964.

Briggs, John W. "Italians in Italy and America: A Study of Change Within Community from Immigrants to Three American Cities, 1890-1930." Ph.D. Dissertation, University of Minnesota, 1972.

Cerase, Francesco P. "From Italy to the United States and Back: Returned Migrants, Conservative or Innovative?" Ph.D. dissertation, Columbia University, 1971.

Chazanoff, William. "The Sicilians of Fredonia."Ph.D. dissertation, State University of New York, Fredonia, 1961.

Davis, Lawrence B. "The Baptist Response to Immigration in the United States, 1880-1925." Ph.D. dissertation, University of Rochester, 1968.

DeBilio, Francis D. "Protestant Mission Work among Italians in Boston." Ph.D. dissertation, Boston University, 1949.

Fenton, Edwin. "Immigrants and Unions, A Case Study: Italians and American Labor, 1870-1920." Ph.D. thesis, Harvard University, 1957.

Ferroni, Charles D. "The Italians in Cleveland: A Study in Assimilation." Ph.D. dissertation, Kent State University, 1969.

Finestone, Harold. "A Comparative Study of Reformation and Recidivism Among Italian and Polish Criminal Offenders." Ph.D. dissertation, University of Chicago, 1964.

Gartner, Carol B. "A New Mirror for America: Fiction of the Immigrant of the Ghetto, 1890-1930." Ph.D. dissertation, New York University, 1970.

Gilkey, George R. "The Effects of Emigration on Italy, 1900-1923." Ph.D. dissertation, Northwestern University, 1950.

Hoffman, George. "Catholic Immigrant Aid Societies in New York City, 1880-1920." Ph.D. dissertation, St. John's University, 1947.

Iorizzo, Luciano. "Italian Immigration and the Impact of the Padrone System." Ph.D. dissertation, Syracuse University, 1966.

Krall, Dorothy R. (Newman). "The Second Generation Immigrant in America with Special Reference to Problems of Adjustment." Ph.D. dissertation, Yale University, 1937.

Linkh, Richard M. "Catholicism and the European Immigrant, 1900-1924, A Chapter in American Catholic School Thought." Ph.D. dissertation, Columbia University, 1973.

LoConte, John. "Franciscan Mission Work Among the Italians of Boston." M.A. thesis, Catholic University of America, 1967.

Mondello, Salvatore A. "The Italian Immigrant in Urban America 1880-1920, as Reported in the Contemporary Periodical Press." Ph.D. dissertation, New York University, 1960.

Perotta, Christopher. "Catholic Care Among Italian Immigrants." Ph.D. dissertation, Catholic University of America, 1925.

Ragucci, Antoinette T. "Generational Continuity and Change in Concepts of Health, Curing Practices, and Ritual Expressions of Women of an Italian-American Enclave." Ph.D. dissertation, Boston University, 1970.

Serino, Gustave R. "Italians in the Political Life of Boston." Ph.D. dissertation, Harvard University. 1950.

Stibili, Edward. "The Italian Saint Raphael Society in America." Ph.D. dissertation, University of Notre Dame, 1977.

Tait, Joseph W. "Some Aspects of the Effect of the Dominant American Culture Upon Children of Italian-Born Parents." Ph.D. dissertation, Columbia University, 1943.

Tomasi, Silvano M. "Assimilation and Religion: The Role of the Italian Ethnic Church in the New York Metropolitan Area, 1880-1930." Ph.D. dissertation, Fordham University, 1972.

Winsey, Valentine R. "A Study of the Effect of Transplantation Upon Attitudes toward the United States of Southern Italians in New York as Revealed by Survivors of the Mass Migration, 1887-1915." Ph.D. dissertation, New York University, 1966.

Zaloha, Anna. "A Study of the Persistence of Italian Customs Among 143 Families of Italian Descent." M.A. thesis, Northwestern University, 1937.

Published Works

Abramson, Harold. *Ethnic Diversity in Catholic America.* New York: John Wiley, 1973.

Acta et decreta concilii plenarii Baltimorensis tertii. Baltimore: National Council of Bishops, 1884.

Action for Boston Community Development. *The Educational Experience of East Boston and the North End: a preliminary report.* Boston, June 16, 1971.

Action for Boston Community Development and United Community Services of Metropolitan Boston. *Five Ethnic Groups in Boston.* Boston, June, 1972.

Adams, Joseph. *In the Italian Quarter of New York.* New York: Arno, 1903.

American Italian Historical Association. *An Inquiry into Organized Crime.* New York, 1970.

––––––. *The Interaction of Italians and Jews in America.* New York, 1974.

––––––. *Italian-American Radicalism.* New York, 1972.

––––––. *Italian Immigrant Women in North America.* New York, 1977.

––––––. *The Religious Experience of Italian Americans.* New York, 1973.

––––––. *The Urban Experience of Italian Americans.* New York, 1975.

––––––. *The United States and Italy: The First Two Hundred Years.* New York, 1976.

Amfitheatrof, Erik. *The Children of Columbus: An Informal History of the Italians in the New World.* Boston: Little Brown, 1972.

Barry, Coleman. *The Catholic Church and German Americans.* Milwaukee: Bruce, 1953.

Bayor, Ronald H. "Italians, Jews and Ethnic Conflict." *International Migration Review* 6 (Winter, 1972): 377-92.

Berkeley, G.F.H. and J. *Italy in the Making.* 3 vols. Cambridge: University Press, 1932.

Boston: A Close-Up of Its Neighborhoods, Its People and Its Problems. Boston: Boston Globe Publications, 1971.

Boston, City of. *A Record of the Streets, Alleys, Places, Etc. of the City of Boston.* Boston: City of Boston Printing Office, 1910.

Boston Herald Traveler Research Department. *Boston: America's Sixth Market: 1950 Census.* Boston: Boston Herald Traveler Publications, 1954.

Boston Redevelopment Authority Planning Department. *North End Recreation and Open Space Study.* City of Boston, Parks and Recreation Department, 1968.

Bushee, Frederick. *Ethnic Factors in the Population of Boston.* New York,: Macmillan, 1903.

Caliaro, Marco and Mario Francesconi. *John Baptist Scalabrini: Apostle to the Emigrants.* New York: Center for Migration Studies, 1977.

Caroli, Betty Boyd. *Italian Repatriation from the United States, 1900-1914.* New York: Center for Migration Studies, 1974.

Carr, John F. *Guide for the Immigrant Italian in the United States.* New York: Arno, 1911.

Cerase, Francesco P. "A Study of Italian Immigrants Returning from the United States of America." *International Migration Review* 1 (Summer, 1967): 67-74.

––––––. "Expectations and Reality: A Case Study of Return Migration from the United States to Southern Italy." *International Migration Review* 8 (Summer, 1974): 245-64.

Chabod, Federico. *Croce Storico.* Torino: Einaudi, 1961.

––––––. *A History of Italian Fascism.* Torino, 1961.

––––––. *L'Italie Contemporanie.* Torino: Einaudi, 1961.

––––––. *Storia della politica estera italiana dal 1870-1896.* Bari: G. Laterza, 1965.

Child, Irvin L. *Italian or American? The Second Generation in Conflict.* New Haven: Yale University Press, 1943.

Circolo Italo-Americano di Boston, an Open Letter from a Member of. Boston, 1908. Staten Island, New York: Center for Migration Studies.

Clark, Francis E. *Our Italian Fellow Citizens in Their Old Homes and Their New*. Boston: Small and Maynard, 1919.

Clough, Shephard Bancroft. *Economic History of Italy*. New York: Columbia Univeristy Press, 1964.

Clough, Shephard Bancroft and Salvatore Saladino. *A History of Modern Italy*. New York: Columbia Unviersity Press, 1968.

Cordasco, Francesco and Eugene Bucchioni. *The Italians: Social Backgrounds of an American Group*. New York: Kelley, 1974.

Croce, Benedetto. *History as Thought and Action*. New York: Russell and Russell, 1938.

_____. *History of Europe in the 19th Century*. London: Allen and Unwin, 1933.

_____. *History of Italy, 1871-1915*. London: Oxford Press, 1929.

_____. *History of the Kindgom of Naples*. Chicago: University of Chicago Press, 1925.

D'Angelo, Pascal. *Son of Italy*. New York: Macmillan, 1924.

Davis, W.H. *The Relation of the Foreign Population to the Mortality Rates of Boston*. 37th Meeting of the American Academy of Medicine. June, 1912.

DeConde, Alexander. *Half Bitter, Half Sweet: An Excursion into Italian-American History*. New York: Scribners, 1971.

Dinnerstein, Leonard and Frederic C. Jaher. *The Aliens: A History of Ethnic Minorities in America*. New York: Appleton, Century, Crofts, 1970.

Dinnerstein, Leonard and David W. Reimers. *Ethnic Americans: A History of Immigration and Assimilation*. New York: Oxford University Press, 1975.

Dolan, Jay B. *The Immigrant Church: New York's Irish and German Catholics, 1815-1865*. Baltimore: Johns Hopkins University Press, 1975.

Dos Passos, John. *Facing the Chair: Sacco and Vanzetti—The Story of the Americanization of Two Foreign Born Workmen*. Boston: Sacco-Vanzetti Defense Committee, 1927.

Drake, Samuel Adams. *Old Landmarks and Historic Personages of Boston*. Boston: Little Brown, 1872.

Dunn, Elizabeth and Sheila Elfman. *Four Areas of Boston, 1970*. Boston: United Community Services, 1973.

Ehrmann, Herbert. *The Case That Would Not Die*. Boston: Little Brown, 1969.

_____. *The Untried Case: The Sacco-Vanzetti Case and the Morelli Gang*. New York: Vanguard, 1960.

Ets, Marie Hall. *Rosa. The Life of an Italian Immigrant*. Minneapolis: University of Minnesota Press, 1970.

Fairchild, Henry Pratt. *The Melting Pot Mistake*. Boston: Little Brown, 1926.

Felici, Icilio. *Father to the Immigrants*. New York: P.J. Kennedy, 1955.

Femminella, Frank. "The Impact of Italian Migration and American Catholicism." *International Migration Digest* 1 (Spring, 1964): 21-24.

Fenton, Edwin. *Immigrants and Unions*. New York: Arno, 1957.

Feuhrlicht, Roberta Strauss. *Justice Crucified*. New York: Harcourt Brace, 1977.

Firey, Walter. *Land Use in Central Boston*. New York: Greenwood Press, 1968.

Foerster, Robert F. *Italian Emigration of Our Times*. New York: Arno, 1919,

Frangini, A. *Italiani in Boston, Massachusetts*. Boston: Stamperia Commerciale, 1907.

Frankfurter, Felix. *The Case of Sacco and Vanzetti*. New York: Grosset and Dunlap, 1962.

Gambino, Richard. *Blood of My Blood: The Dilemma of the Italian-Americans*. Garden City: Doubleday, 1974.

_____. *Vendetta: A True Story of the Worst Lynching in America: The Mass Murder of Italian Americans in New Orleans in 1891, the Vicious Motivations Behind It and the Repurcussions that Linger to this Day*. New York: Doubleday, 1977.

Gans, Herbert J. *The Urban Villagers.* New York: Macmillan, 1962.

Gellart, John C. *The Growth and Development of Italian Children.* New York: Arno, 1924.

Grant, Madison. *The Passing of the Great Race.* New York: Arno, 1916.

Greeley, Andrew. *Why Can't They Be Like Us: America's White Ethnic Groups.* New York: E.P. Dutton, 1970.

Griel, Cecile. *I Problemi della Madre in Un Paese Nuovo.* New York, 1919.

Hales, E.E.Y. *Pio Nono.* New York: P.J. Kennedy, 1954.

Halperin, S. William. *Italy and the Vatican at War.* Chicago: University of Chicago Press, 1939.

Handlin, Oscar. *Boston's Immigrants.* Cambridge: Harvard University Press, 1941.

———. *Children of the Uprooted.* New York, 1966.

———. *The Uprooted: The Migrations That Made the American People.* Boston: Little Brown, 1951.

Harney, Robert F. " 'Chiaroscuro' Italians in Toronto 1885-1915." *Italian Americana* 1 (Spring, 1975): 143-68.

———. "Italian Sojourners of the Northwest," *American Italian Historical Association Proceedings,* October 1978.

Hartwell, Edward, et al. *Boston and Its Story, 1630-1915.* Boston: City of Boston Printing Office, 1916.

Hentze, Margot. *Pre-Fascist Italy.* London, 1939.

Herlihy, Elizabeth M., ed., *Fifty Years of Boston.* Boston, 1932.

Higham, John. "American Immigration Policy in Historical Perspective." *Law and Contemporary Problems* 22 (Spring, 1956): 213-35.

Hibbert, Christopher. *Garibaldi and His Enemies.* Boston: Little Brown, 1965.

Howard, Brett. *Boston: A Social History.* New York: Hawthorn, 1976.

Howe, Irving. *World of Our Fathers: The Journey of the East European Jews to America and the Life They Found and Made.* New York: Simon and Schuster, 1976.

Iorizzo, Luciano, and Salvatore Mondello. "Origins of Italian-American Criminality: From New Orleans Through Prohibition." *Italian Americana.* 1 (Spring, 1975): 217-36.

Italian Baptist Missionary Association. *Report of the Committee on Americanization.* New York, 1918.

"Italians in Boston." *Charities* 12 (1904): 451-42.

Jones, Maldwyn A. *American Immigration.* (Chicago: University of Chicago Press), 1960.

Juliani, Richard N. "American Voices, Italian Accents: The Perception of Social Conditions and Personal Motives by Immigrants." *Italian Americana* (Autumn, 1974): 1-26.

Kennedy, John F. *A Nation of Immigrants.* New York: Harper and Row, 1964.

Kessner, Thomas. *The Golden Door: Italian and Jewish Immigrant Mobility in New York City, 1880-1915.* New York: Oxford University Press, 1977.

King, Moses. *King's Handbook of Boston.* Boston: Moses King, 1878.

Koren, John. "The Padrone System and Padrone Banks." United States Department of Labor Bulletin 9 (March, 1897).

LaGumina, Salvatore J. "Ethnicity in American Political Life—The Italian American Experience." *International Migration Review* 3 (Fall, 1968): 78-81.

———. *Wop.* San Francisco: Straight Arrow Books, 1973.

Langtry, Albert P., ed. *Metropolitan Boston: A Modern History.* 5 vol. New York: Lewis Historical Building Company, 1929.

LaPiana, George. *The Italians of Milwaukee.* Milwaukee, 1915.

Levi, Carlo. *Christ Stopped at Eboli.* New York: Noonday Press, 1947.

Levine, Louis. *The Women's Garment Workers.* New York, 1924.

Linkh, Richard M. *American Catholicism and European Immigrants.* New York: Center for Migration Studies, 1975.

List of Members of the Italy America Society. March, 1920. New York, 1920.

Lopreato, Joseph. *Italian Americans.* New York: Random House, 1970.

Lord, Robert H., John E. Sexton, and Edmund T. Harrington. *History of the Archdiocese of Boston.* New York: Sheed and Ward, 1944.

Lyons, Eugene. *The Life and Death of Sacco and Vanzetti.* New York: International Publishers, 1927.

Mangano, Antonio. *The Italian Colonies of New York City.* New York, 1903.

———. *Sons of Italy.* New York: Ozer, 1917.

———. *Religious Work Among Italians in America.* Philadelphia: Protestant Evangelical Publication, 1917.

Martellone, Anna Maria. *"Una Little Italy nell'Atene D'America."* Napoli: Guida Editori, 1973.

Martin, George. *The Red Shirt and the Cross of Savoy.* New York: Dodd Mead, 1969.

Mariano, John H. *The Italian Immigrant and our Courts.* Boston: American Press, 1925.

Masini, Pier Carlo. *Storia degli anarchici italiani da Bakunin a Malatesta.* Milano: Rizzoli, 1969.

Mastro-Valerio, Alessandro. *Remarks Upon the Italian Colony of Chicago.* Chicago, 1895.

McBride, Paul W. "The Italian-Americans and the Catholic Church: Old and New Perspectives." *Italian Americana* 1 (Spring, 1975): 265-80.

Mead, Margaret. "Group Intelligence Tests and Linguistic Disability Among Italian Children." *School and Society* 25 (April 16, 1927): 465-68.

Merwick, Donna. *Boston Priests, 1848-1910: A Study of Intellectual and Social Change.* Cambridge: Harvard University Press, 1973.

Moffat, Adelene. *"Exhibition of Italian Arts and Crafts in Boston."* *Survey* 22 (1909): 51-57.

Mondello, Salvatore and Luciano Iorizzo. *The Italian Americans.* New York: Twayne, 1971.

Moss, Leonard, and Walter Thomson. "The South Italian Family: Literature and Observation." *Human Organization* 18 (Spring, 1959): 35-41.

Moynihan, Daniel Patrick and Nathan Glazer. *Beyond the Melting Pot: The Negroes, Puerto Ricans, Jews, Italians, and Irish of New York City.* (Cambridge: Massachusetts Institute of Technology Press), 1959.

Nelli, Humbert S. *"Italians and Crime in Chicago: The Formative Years 1890-1920."* *American Journal of Sociology* 74 (January, 1969): 373-91.

———. *The Italians in Chicago, 1880-1930: A Study in Ethnic Mobility.* New York, 1973.

———. "Italians in Urban America: A Study in Ethnic Adjustment." *International Migration Review* 1 (Summer, 1967): 38-55.

———. "The Italian Padrone System in the United States." *Labor History* 5 (Spring, 1964): 153-67.

Novak, Michael. *The Rise of the Unmeltable Ethnics.* New York: Macmillan, 1972.

O'Connor, Thomas H. *Bibles, Brahmins and Bosses: A Short History of Boston.* Boston: Boston Public Library, 1976.

Oppenheimer, Francis J. *The Truth About the Black Hand.* New York: A.C. Boni, 1909.

Paul Revere Memorial Association. *Boston Handbook.* Boston, 1950.

Pirazzini, Agide. *Training an Italian Missionary for America.* New York, 1918.

Pomeroy, Sarah G. *The Italians.* New York: Arno, 1914.

Riis, Jacob. *The Battle with the Slum.* New York: Macmillan, 1902.

———. *Children of the Tenements.* New York: Macmillan, 1906.

———. *How the Other Half Lives.* New York, 1890: Belknap Press Edition, 1976.

Robertson, Alexander. *Mussolini and the New Italy.* London: H.R. Allenson, 1929.

Rolle, Andrew F. *The Immigrant Upraised: Italian Adventurers and Colonists in an Expanding America.* Norman: University of Oklahoma Press, 1968.

Rose, Philip M. *The Italians in America.* New York: Doran, 1922.

Salamone, A. William. *Italian Democracy in the Making, 1900-1914.* Philadelphia: University of Pennsylvania Press, 1945.

Salvadori, Massimo. *Cavour and the Unification of Italy.* New York: Van Nostrand, 1961.
_____. *A Pictorial History of the Italian People.* New York: Crown, 1972.
Salvatorelli, Luigi. *A Concise History of Italy.* New York: Oxford, 1940.
_____. *Risorgimento: pensiero e azione.* Torino: Einaude, 1960.
Salvemini, Gaetano. *Italian Fascist Activities in the United States.* New York: Center for Migration Studies, 1977.
Sarfatti, Margherita G. *The Life of Benito Mussolini.* New York: Frederick Stokes, 1925.
Saveth, Edward N. *American Historians and European Immigrants, 1875-1925.* New York: Arno, 1948.
Schiavo, Giovanni E. *Four Centuries of Italian American History.* New York: Arno, 1958.
_____. *The Italians in Chicago,* (Chicago: The Italian American Publishing Company), 1928.
Schneider, Herbert. *Making the Fascist State.* New York, 1928.
_____. *Making Fascists.* New York, 1929.
Scudder, Vida. *Experiments in Fellowship: Work with Italians in Boston.* Boston: Houghton Mifflin, 1909.
Seton-Watson, Christopher. *Italy from Liberalism to Fascism, 1870-1925.* London: Oxford Press, 1967.
Sforza, Count Carlo. *Contemporary Italy.* New York, 1944.
Sheridan, Frank. *Gl'Italiani negli Stati Uniti.* Roma, 1909.
Shurtleff, Nathaniel Bradstreet. *A Topographical and Historical Description of Boston.* Boston: A Williams and Company, 1870.
Smith, Dennis Mack. *Cavour and Garibaldi, 1860: A Study in Political Conflict.* Cambridge: University Press, 1954.
_____. *Italy, A Modern History.* 2 vol. London: Oxford University Press, 1959.
Solomon, Barbara. *Ancestors and Immigrants: A Changing New England Tradition.* Cambridge: Harvard University Press, 1956.
Southworth, Michael and Susan. *Boston 200 Discovery Network: North End Survey.* Privately published, updated. Available at Boston Public Library, North End Branch.
Speranza, Gino. *Race or Nation: Conflict of Divided Loyalties.* Indianapolis, 1925.
Stark, James H. *Stark's Antique Views of ye Towne of Boston.* Boston: Morse-Pierce Company, 1907.
Stella, Antonio. *Some Aspects of Italian Emigration to the United States.* New York: Arno, 1924.
_____. *The Effects of Urban Congestion on Italian Women and Children.* New York: Arno, 1908.
Sturzo, Luigi. *Italy and Fascism.* London, 1926.
Sullivan, James. *The Catholic Church in New England.* Boston: Holy Cross Press, 1895.
Tasca, Angelo. *Origins of Fascism in Italy, 1918-1922.* London, 1938.
Tessarolo, Giulivo. *The Church's Magna Charta for Migrants.* New York: Center for Migration Studies, 1962.
Thayer, John A. *Italy and the Great War.* Madison: University of Wisconsin Press, 1964.
Thayer, William Roscoe. *The Dawn of Italian Independence, 1814-1849.* 2 vol. Boston: Little Brown, 1893.
_____. *The Life and Times of Cavour.* 2 vol. Boston: Little Brown, 1914.
This is the North End. Boston: The Italian News Publishing Company, 1956.
Therstrom, Stephan. *The Other Bostonians: Poverty and Progress in the American Metropolis, 1880-1970.* Cambridge: Harvard University Press, 1973.
_____. *Poverty and Progress in the 19th Century.* Cambridge: Harvard University Press, 1964.
Thomas, Norman. *Six Years in Little Italy.* New York: Norton, 1918.
Todisco, Paula J. *Boston's First Neighborhood: The North End.* Boston: Boston Public Library, 1976.

Tomasi, Lydio F. *The Italian American Family*. New York: Center for Migration Studies, 1974.
_____. *The Italian in America: The Progressive View, 1891-1914*. New York: Center for Migration Studies, 1973.
Tomasi, Lydio F. and M.H. Engels, eds. *The Italian Experience in the United States*. New York: Center for Migration Studies, 1970.
Tomasi, Silvano. *Piety and Power*. New York: Center for Migration Studies, 1975.
Tomasi, S. and C.B. Keely. *Whom Have We Welcomed? The Adequacy and Quality of United States Immigration Data for Policy Analysis and Evaluation*. New York: Center for Migration Studies, 1975.
Trevelyan, George MaCauley. *Garibaldi and the Making of Italy*. London: Longmans Green, 1911.
_____. *Garibaldi and the Thousand*. London: Longmans Green, 1909.
_____. *Garibaldi's Defense of the Roman Republic*. London: Longmans Green, 1909.
Vecoli, Rudolph J. "Contadini in Chicago: A Critique of *The Uprooted.*" *Journal of American History* 51 (December, 1964): 404-16.
_____. "Italian Immigrants and the Catholic Church." *Journal of Social History* 2 (Spring, 1969): 217-67.
Villari, Luigi. *The Fascist Experiment*. London, 1926.
_____. *Gli Stati Uniti d'America e l'emigrazione Italiane*. Milano, 1912.
Warner, Sam B. Jr. *Streetcar Suburbs: The Process of Growth in Boston, 1870-1900*. Cambridge: Harvard University Press, 1962.
_____. *The Way We Really Live: Social Change in Boston Since 1920*. Boston: Boston Public Library, 1977.
Weider, Arnold A. *The Early Jewish Community of Boston's North End*. Waltham, Mass.: Brandeis University Press, 1962.
Wenk, Michael, ed. *Pieces of a Dream*. New York: Center for Migration Studies, 1972.
Whitehill, Walter Muir. *Boston, A Topographical History*. Cambridge: Harvard University Press, 1959.
_____. *Boston, Portrait of a City*. Barre, Mass.: Barre Publishers, 1964.
Whyte, William F. "Race Conflicts in the North End of Boston." *New England Quarterly* 12 (December, 1939): 623-24.
_____. "Social Organization and the Slums." *American Sociological Review* 8 (February, 1943): 34-39.
Wittke, Carl. *We Who Built America: The Saga of the Immigrant*. New York, 1939.
Woods, Robert. *Americans in Process*. Boston: Houghton Mifflin, 1903.
_____. *The City Wilderness*. Boston: Houghton Mifflin, 1898.
_____. "Notes on the Italians in Boston." *Charities* 12 (May 7, 1904): 541-42.
Woods, Robert and Albert J. Kennedy. *Zones of Emergence*. Cambridge: Harvard University Press, 1907.

Index